Illustrated
LONDON

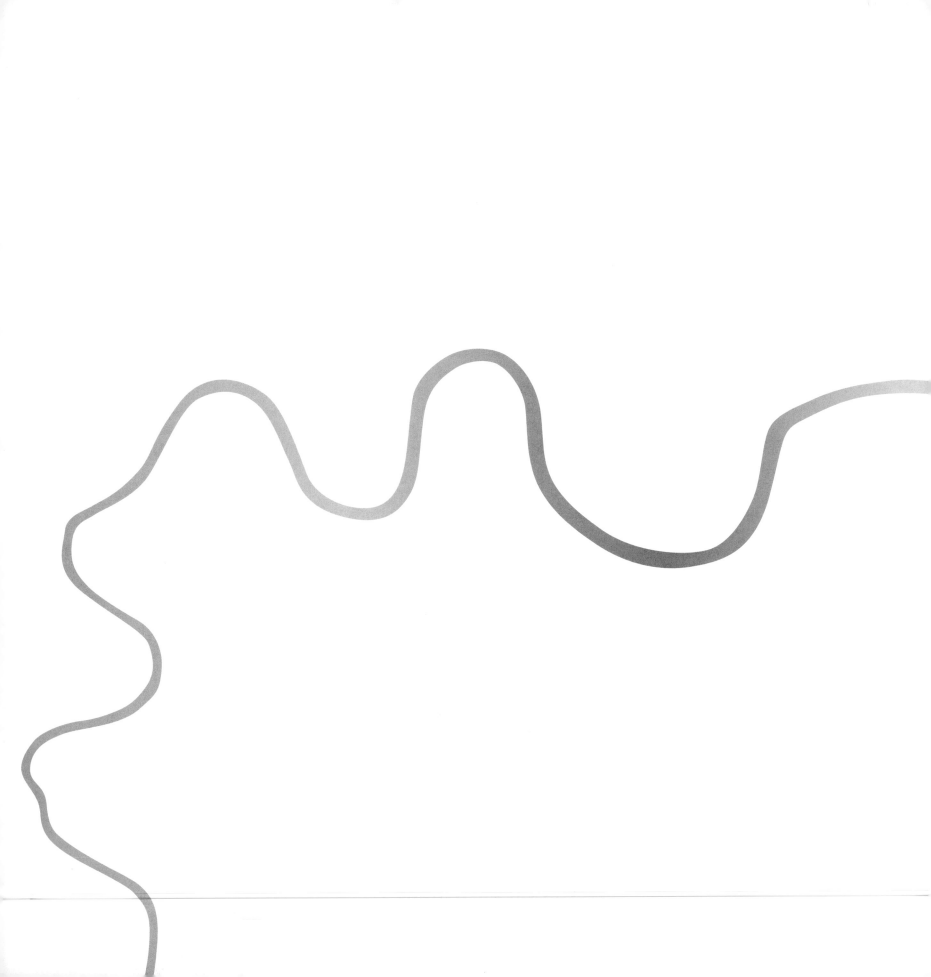

Illustrated
LONDON

PETER ACKROYD

Chatto & Windus
LONDON

Published by Chatto & Windus 2003
2 4 6 8 10 9 7 5 3

London The Biography first published in Great Britain in 2000 by Chatto & Windus
This edition, *Illustrated London* first published in Great Britain in 2003 by Chatto & Windus
Random House, 20 Vauxhall Bridge Road, London SW1V 2SA

Random House Australia (Pty) Limited 20 Alfred Street, Milsons Point, Sydney, New South Wales
2061, Australia

Random House New Zealand Limited 18 Poland Road, Glenfield, Auckland 10, New Zealand

Random House South Africa (Pty) Limited Endulini, 5A Jubilee Road, Parktown 2193, South Africa

The Random House Group Limited Reg. No. 954009
www.randomhouse.co.uk

A CIP catalogue record for this book is available from the British Library

ISBN 0 7011 7613 X

A HERE+THERE production for Chatto & Windus
Design & Art Direction: Caz Hildebrand
Picture Editor: Lily Richards
www.hereandtheregroup.com

Papers used by Random House are natural, recyclable products made from wood grown in sustainable
forests; the manufacturing processes conform to the environmental regulations of the country of origin

Printed and bound by Appl Druck, Wemding, Germany

For
Iain Johnston
and
Frederick Nicholas Robertson

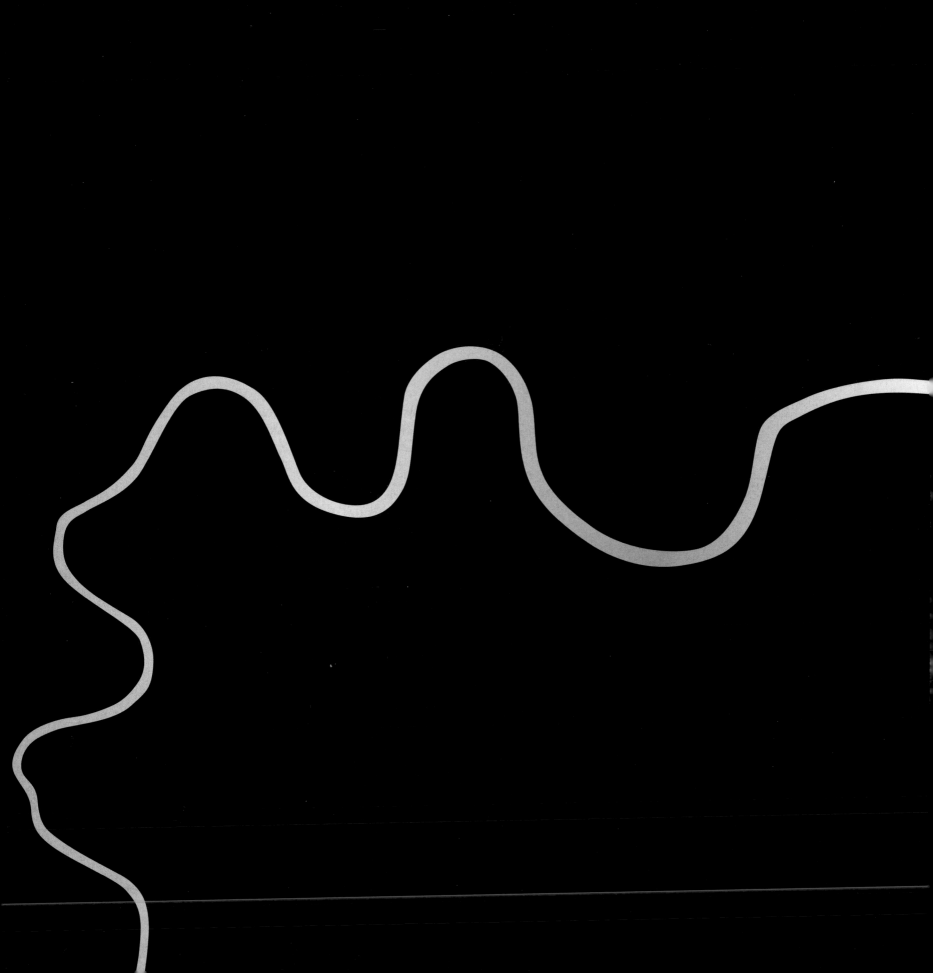

contents

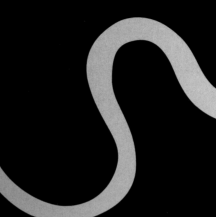

in the beginn

ng was the sea: the site of the capital was covered by great waters.

If you were to touch the plinth upon which the equestrian statue of King Charles I is placed, at Charing Cross, your fingers might rest upon the projecting fossils of sea lilies, starfish or sea urchins. There is a photograph of that statue taken in 1839; with its small boys in stove-pipe hats the scene already seems remote, and so how unimaginably distant lies the life of those tiny marine creatures. Yet in the beginning was the sea: the site of the capital was covered by great waters.

London has always been a vast ocean in which survival is not certain. Like the sea and the gallows, London refuses nobody. Those who venture upon its currents look for prosperity or fame, even if they often founder in its depths. The dome of St Paul's has been seen trembling upon a 'vague troubled sea' of fog, while dark streams of people flow over London Bridge, or Waterloo Bridge, and emerge as torrents in the narrow thoroughfares of London. The social workers of the mid-nineteenth century spoke of rescuing 'drowning' people in Whitechapel or Shoreditch. If you look from a distance, you observe a sea of roofs, and have no more knowledge of the dark streams of people than of the denizens of some unknown ocean. But the city is always a heaving and restless place, with its own torrents and billows, its foam and spray. The sound of its streets is like the murmur from a sea shell. The real confluence, however, lies in this – that London, for so long the arbiter of trade and of the sea, should have upon its fabric the silent signature of the tides and waves.

And when the waters parted, the London earth was revealed. In 1877, in a characteristically grand example of Victorian engineering, a vast well was taken down 1,146 feet at the southern end of Tottenham Court Road. It travelled hundreds of millions of years, touching the primeval landscapes of this city site, and from its evidence we can list the layers beneath our feet from the Devonian to the Jurassic and the Cretaceous. Above these strata lie 650 feet of chalk, outcrops of which can be seen upon the Downs or the Chilterns as the rim of the London Basin, that shallow saucer-like declivity in which the city rests. On top of the chalk itself lies the thick London clay which is in turn covered by deposits of gravel and brick-earth. Here, then, is the making of the city in more than one sense; the clay and the chalk and the brick-earth have for almost two thousand years been employed to construct the houses and public buildings of London. It is almost as if the city raised itself from its primeval origin, creating a human settlement from the senseless material of past time.

This was not, even then, an unpeopled region. Within the bones of the King's Cross mammoth were also found pieces of a flint hand-axe which can be dated to the Palaeolithic period. We can say with some certainty that for half a million years there has been in London a pattern of habitation and hunting if not of settlement. The first great fire of London was started, a quarter of a million years ago, in the forests south of the Thames. That river had by then taken its appointed course but not its later appearance; it was very broad, fed by many streams, occluded by forests, bordered by swamps and marshes.

A great gathering of flint tools, excavated in Southwark, is assumed to mark the remains of a Mesolithic manufactory; a hunting camp of the same period has been discovered upon Hampstead Heath. On these ancient sites have been found pits and post-holes,

St Paul's Cathedral during the Blitz, attesting to its miraculous survival amid the flames. 'No one who saw will ever forget their emotions on the night when London was burning and the dome seemed to ride the sea of fire.'

together with human remains and evidence of feasting. These early people drank a potion similar to mead or beer. Like their London descendants, they left vast quantities of rubbish everywhere. Like them, too, they met for the purposes of worship. For many thousands of years these ancient peoples treated the great river as a divine being to be placated, and surrendered to its depths the bodies of their illustrious dead.

In the late Neolithic period there appeared, from the generally marshy soil on the northern bank of the Thames, twin hills covered by gravel and brick-earth, surrounded by sedge and willow. They were forty to fifty feet in height, and were divided by a valley through which flowed a stream. We know them as Cornhill and Ludgate Hill, with the now buried Walbrook running between. Thus emerged London.

In those long stretches of time designated as the 'Late Bronze Age' and the 'Early Iron Age' – a period spanning almost a thousand years – shards and fragments of bowls, and pots, and tools, were left all over London. There are signs of prehistoric activity in the areas now known as St Mary Axe and Gresham Street, Austin Friars and Finsbury Circus, with altogether some 250 'finds' clustered in the area of the twin hills together with Tower Hill and Southwark. From the Thames itself many hundreds of metal objects have been retrieved, while along its banks is to be found frequent evidence of metal-working. This is the period from which the great early legends of London spring. It is also, in its latter phase, the age of the Celts.

In the first century BC, Julius Caesar's description of the region around London suggests the presence of an elaborate, rich and well-organised tribal civilisation. Its population was 'exceedingly large' and 'the ground thickly studded with homesteads'. There is every reason to suppose that this area of the Thames was a centre of commerce and of industry, with a market in iron products as well as elaborate workings in bronze, with merchants from Gaul, Rome and Spain bringing Samian ware, wine and spices in exchange for corn, metals and slaves.

In the history of this period completed by Geoffrey of Monmouth in 1136, the principal city in the island of Britain is undoubtedly London. It is believed by historians of early Britain that a people known as the Trinovantes settled on territory to the north of the London region. Curiously enough, Geoffrey states that the first name of the city was Trinovantum. He also mentions the presence of temples within London itself; even if they had existed, these palisades and wooden enclosures would since have been lost.

But nothing is wholly lost. Tokens and traces of a Celtic or Druidic London were thoroughly examined and were found significant.

One of the earliest maps of Britain, drawn by Matthew Paris in the middle of the thirteenth century.

The fact that existing street names may betray a Celtic origin – Colin Deep Lane, Pancras Lane, Maiden Lane, Ingal Road among them – is also instructive. Long-forgotten trackways, too, have guided the course of modern thoroughfares; the crossroads at the Angel, Islington, for example, marks the point where two prehistoric British roads intersected.

There is no more suspect or difficult subject, in the context of this period, than Druidism.

It has been suggested that the London area was controlled from three sacred mounds; they are named as Penton Hill, Tothill and the White Mound, otherwise known as Tower Hill. It is known that in prehistoric worship a holy place was marked by a spring, a grove and a well or ritual shaft. Interestingly, there is a reference to a 'shrubby maze' in the pleasure gardens of White Conduit House, situated on the high ground of Pentonville, and a maze's avatar was a sacred hill or grove. Close at hand is the famous well of Sadler's Wells. Another maze was to be found in the area once known as Tothill Fields in Westminster. Here also is a sacred spring, deriving from the 'holy well' in Dean's Yard, Westminster. A fair, similar to the pleasure gardens upon White Conduit Fields, was established here at an early date; the first extant reference is dated 1257.

Here, then, is the hypothesis: London mounds, which bear so many similar characteristics, are in fact the holy sites of Druid ritual. The maze is the sacred equivalent of the oak grove, while the wells and springs represent the worship of the god of the water. Pleasure gardens and fairs are more recent versions of those prehistoric festivals or meetings which were held upon the same ground. So antiquaries have named Tothill, Penton and Tower Hill as the holy places of London.

It is equally important to look for evidence of continuity. In the records of St Paul's Cathedral the adjacent buildings are known as 'Camera Dianae'. A fifteenth-century chronicler recalled a time when 'London worships Diana', the goddess of the hunt, which is at least one explanation for the strange annual ceremony that took place at St Paul's as late as the sixteenth century. There, in the Christian temple erected on the sacred site of Ludgate Hill, a stag's head was impaled upon a spear and carried about the church; it was then received upon the steps of the church by priests wearing garlands of flowers upon their heads. So the pagan customs of London survived into recorded history, just as a latent paganism survived among the citizens themselves.

One other inheritance from prehistoric worship may also be considered. The sense of certain places as being powerful or venerable was taken over by the Christians in the recognition of 'holy wells' and in such ceremonies of territorial piety as 'beating the bounds'. Yet the same sensibility is to be found in the writings of the great London visionaries, from William Blake to Arthur Machen, writings in which the city itself is considered to be a sacred place with its own joyful and sorrowful mysteries.

In this Celtic period, which lurks like some chimera in the shadows of the known world, the great legends of London find their origin. Brutus, in legend the founder of the city, was buried within London's walls. Locrinus kept his lover, Estrildis, in a secret chamber beneath the ground. Bladud, who practised sorcery, constructed a pair of wings with which to fly through the air of London; yet he fell against the roof of the Temple of Apollo situated in the very heart of the city, perhaps on Ludgate Hill itself. From this period, too, came the narratives of Lear and of Cymbeline. More powerful still is the legend of the giant Gremagot who by some strange alchemy was transformed into the twins Gog and Magog, who became tutelary spirits of London. It has often been suggested that each of this characteristically ferocious pair, whose statues have stood for many centuries within the Guildhall, guards one of the twin hills of London.

Such stories are recorded by John Milton in *The History of Britain*, published a little more than three hundred years ago. 'After this, Brutus in a chosen place builds Troia nova, chang'd in time to Trinovantum, now London: and began to enact Laws.' Brutus was the great-grandson of Aeneas who, some years after the fall of Troy, led the exodus of Trojans from Greece; in the course of his exilic wanderings he was granted a dream in which the goddess Diana spoke words of prophecy to him: an island far to the west, beyond the realm of Gaul, 'fitts thy people'; you are to sail there, Brutus, and establish a city which will become another Troy. 'And Kings be born of thee, whose dredded might shall aw the World, and Conquer Nations bold.' London is to maintain a world empire but, like ancient Troy, it may suffer some perilous burning. It is interesting that paintings of London's Great Fire in 1666 make specific allusion to the fall of Troy. This is indeed the central myth of London's origin which can be found in the sixth-century verses of 'Tallisen', where the British are celebrated as the living remnant of Troy, as well as in the later poetry of Edmund Spenser and of Alexander Pope.

Some scholars believe that we can date the wanderings of the apparently legendary Brutus to the period around 1100 BC. In contemporary historiographical terms this marks the period of the Late Bronze Age when new bands or tribes of settlers occupied the area around London; they constructed large defensive enclosures and maintained a heroic life of mead-halls, ring-giving and furious fighting which found expression in later legends. In the waters of the Thames was found a black two-handled cup; its provenance lies in Asia Minor,

London Stone, the magical rock of London.

with an approximate date of 900 BC. So there is some indication of trade between western Europe and the eastern Mediterranean. At the beginning of any civilisation there are fables and legends; only at the end are they proved to be accurate.

One token of Brutus and his Trojan fleet may still remain. If you walk east down Cannon Street, on the other side from the railway station, you will find an iron grille set within the Bank of China. It protects a niche upon which has been placed a stone roughly two feet in height, bearing a faint groove mark upon its top. This is London Stone. For many centuries it was popularly believed to be the stone of Brutus, brought by him as a deity. 'So long as the stone of Brutus is safe,' ran one city proverb, 'so long shall London flourish.' Certainly the stone is of great antiquity; the first reference to it was discovered by John Stow in a 'fair written Gospel book' once belonging to Ethelstone, an early tenth-century king of the West Saxons, where certain lands and rents are 'described to lie near unto London stone'. According to the Victorian County History it originally marked the very centre of the old city, but in 1742 was taken from the middle of Cannon Street and placed within the fabric of St Swithin's Church opposite. There it remained until the Second World War; although a German bomb entirely destroyed the church in 1941, London Stone remained intact.

Its actual significance, however, remains unclear. Some antiquaries have considered it to be a token of civic assembly, connected with the repayment of debts, while others believe it to be a Roman milliarium or milestone. Christopher Wren argued, however, that it possessed too large a foundation for the latter purpose. A judicial role is more likely. That it became a highly venerated object is not in doubt. William Blake was convinced that it marked the site of Druid executions, whose sacrificial victims 'groan'd aloud on London Stone', but its uses were perhaps less melancholy.

When the popular rebel Jack Cade stormed London in 1450, he and his followers

The Tower of London, with the ships on the silver river. One of the first 'views' of London.

De nouuelles dalbion
Il vous en plaust escouter
mon frere et mon copaignon
Alchez qua mon retorner
Ay este deca la mer
Escu a ioyeuse chiere

made their way to the Stone; he touched it with his sword and then exclaimed: 'Now is Mortimer' – this was the name he had assumed – 'lord of this city!' The first mayor of London, in the late twelfth century, was Henry Fitz-Ailwin de Londonestone. It seems likely, therefore, that this ancient object came somehow to represent the power and authority of the city. It sits now, blackened and disregarded, by the side of a busy thoroughfare; over and around it have flowed wooden carts, carriages, sedan chairs, hansom cabs, cabriolets, hackney cabs, omnibuses, bicycles, trams and cars. It was once London's guardian spirit, and perhaps it is still.

Henry Fitz-Ailwin, the first Lord Mayor.

A section of the original London Wall, with medieval additions, can still be seen by Trinity Place just north of the Tower of London; part of the Tower itself was incorporated within the fabric of the wall. It was almost ten feet wide at its base, and more than twenty feet in height. Beside these relics can be seen the stone outline of an inner tower, which contained a wooden staircase leading to a parapet that looked east across the marshes.

From here the spectral wall, the wall as once it was, can be traversed in the imagination. It proceeds north to Cooper's Row, where a section can still be seen in the courtyard of an empty building. It goes through the concrete and marble of the building, then on through the brick and iron of the Fenchurch Street Station viaduct until an extant section rises again in America Square. It is concealed within the basement of a modern building which itself has parapets, turrets and square towers; a strip of glazed red tiling bears more than a passing resemblance to the courses of flat red tiles placed in the ancient Roman structure. It moves through Vine Street (in the car park at No. 35 is a security camera on the ancient line of the now invisible wall), towards Jewry Street, which itself follows the line of the wall almost exactly until it meets Aldgate; all the buildings here can be said to comprise a new wall, separating west from east.

The steps of the subway at Aldgate lead down to a level which was once that of late medieval London, but we follow the wall down Duke's Place and into Bevis Marks. Near the intersection of these two thoroughfares there is now part of that 'ring of steel' which is designed once more to protect the city. On a sixteenth-century map Bevis Marks was aligned to the course of the wall, and it is so still; the pattern of the streets here has been unchanged for many hundreds of years. At the corner of Bevis Marks and St Mary Axe rises a building of white marble with massive vertical windows; a great golden eagle can be seen above its entrance, as if it were part of some imperial standard. Security cameras once more trace the line of the wall, as it leads down Camomile Street towards Bishopsgate and Wormwood

The Tower of London recreated for Stow's Survey of London, first published in 1598.

Street.

It drops beneath the churchyard of St Botolph's, behind a building faced with white stone and curtain-walling of dark glass, but then fragments of it arise beside the church of All Hallows on the Wall, which has been built, in the ancient fashion, to protect and bless these defences. The modern thoroughfare here becomes known, at last, as London Wall. A tower like a postern of brown stone rises above 85 London Wall, very close to the spot where a fourth-century bastion was only recently found. Bethlehem Hospital, or Bedlam, was once built against the north side of the wall; but that, too, has disappeared. Yet it is impossible not to feel the presence or force of the wall as you walk down this straightened thoroughfare which can be dated to the later period of the Roman occupation. A new London Wall then opens up after Moorgate, built over the ruins of the Second World War. The bombs themselves effectively uncovered long-buried remnants of the ancient wall, and stretches both of Roman and medieval origin can still be seen covered with grass and moss. But these old stones are flanked by the glittering marble and polished stone of the new buildings that dominate the city.

Around the site of the great Roman fort, at the north-west angle of the wall, there now arise these new fortresses and towers: Roman House, Britannic Tower, City Tower, Alban Gate and the concrete and granite towers of the Barbican, which have once more brought a sublime bareness and brutality to that area where the Roman legions were sequestered. Even the walkways of this great expanse are approximately the same height as the parapets of the old city wall.

The wall then turns south, and long sections of it can still be seen on the western side

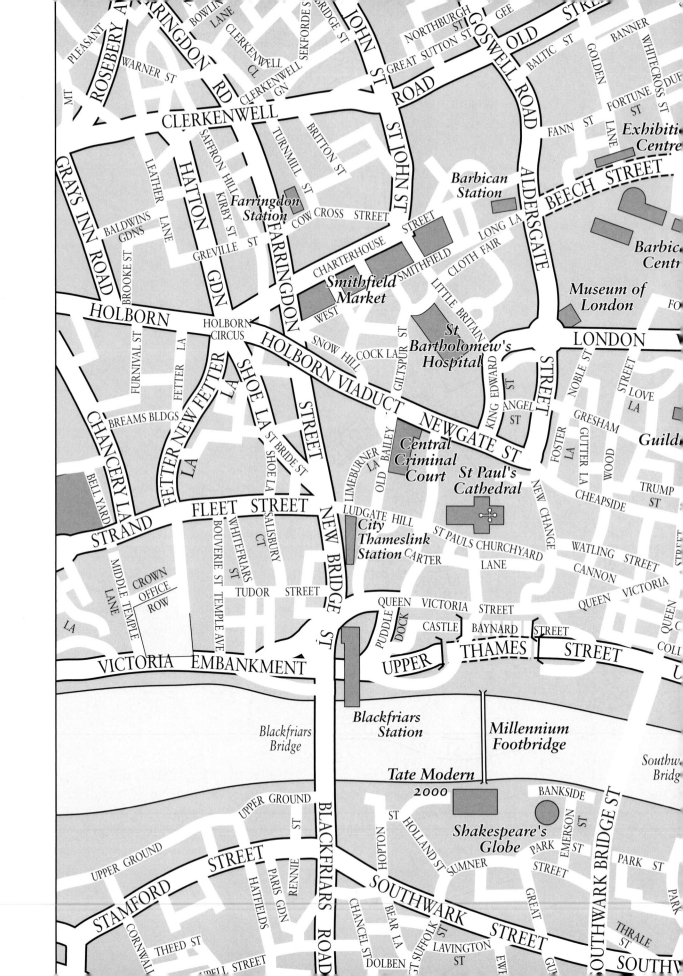

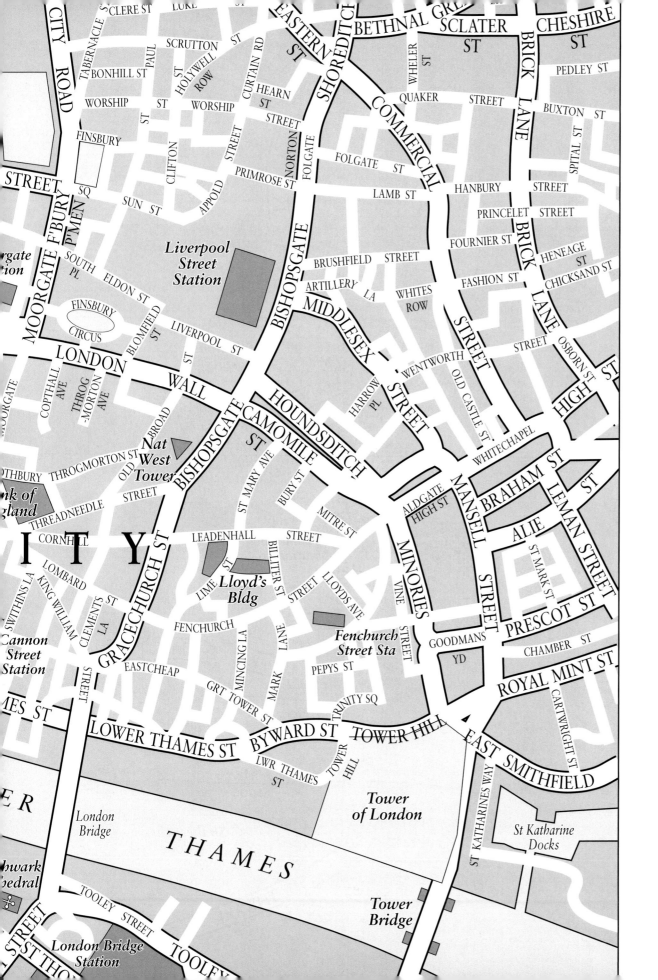

sloping down towards Aldersgate. For most of its course from Aldersgate to Newgate and then to Ludgate, it remains invisible, but there are suggestive tokens of its progress. The great beast of classical antiquity, the Minotaur, has been sculpted just to its north in Postman's Park. The mottled and darkened blocks of the Sessions House beside the Old Bailey still mark the outer perimeter of the wall's defences, and in Amen Court a later wall looking on the back of the Old Bailey is like some revenant of brick and mortar. From the rear of St Martin's Ludgate we cross Ludgate Hill, enter Pilgrim Street and walk beside Pageantmaster Court, where now the lines of the Thameslink parallel those once made by the swiftly moving River Fleet, until we reach the edge of the water where the wall once abruptly stopped.

Mordred besieging the Tower of London, from the Romance of the Grail.

The wall enclosed an area of some 330 acres. To walk its perimeter would have taken approximately one hour, and the modern pedestrian will be able to cover the route in the same time. The streets beside it are still navigable and, in fact, the larger part of the wall itself was not demolished until 1760. Until that time the city had the appearance of a fortress, and in the sagas of Iceland it was known as Lundunaborg, 'London Fort'. It was continually being rebuilt, as if the integrity and identity of the city itself depended upon the survival of this ancient stone fabric; churches were erected beside it, and hermits guarded its gates. Even after its demolition the wall still lived; its stone sides were incorporated into churches or other public buildings.

It is often believed that the Roman wall first defined Roman London, but the invaders were in command of London for 150 years before walls were built and, during that long stretch of time, the city itself evolved in particular – sometimes bloody, sometimes fiery – stages. In 55 BC a military force under the command of Caesar invaded Britain, and within a short time compelled the tribes around London to accept Roman hegemony. Almost a hundred years later the Romans returned with a more settled policy of invasion and conquest. The troops may have crossed the river at Westminster, or Southwark, or Wallingford. It is important for this account only that the administrators and commanders finally chose London as their principal place of settlement because of the strategic advantages of the terrain, and the commercial benefits of this riverine location. It seems likely that the invaders understood the significance of the site from the beginning of their occupation. Here was an estuary, served by a double tide. So it became the central point for sea-borne trade in the south of Britain, and the focus for a network of roads which have survived for almost two thousand years.

The outlines of that first city have been revealed by excavation, with two principal streets of gravel running parallel to the river on the eastern hill. The wooden Roman bridge was located approximately one hundred yards east of the first stone London Bridge, span-

A representation of London from the late fifteenth century Nuremberg Chronicle.

ning the area west of St Olav's Church in Southwark and the foot of Rederes (Pudding) Lane upon the northern bank. Half the legends of London arose upon its foundations; miracles were performed, and visions seen, upon the new wooden thoroughfare. Since its sole purpose was to tame the river, it may then have harnessed the power of a god. Yet that god may have been enraged at the stripping of its riverine authority; thus all the intimations of vengeance and destruction invoked by the famous rhyme 'London Bridge is broken down'.

Only a few years after its foundation, which can be approximately dated between AD 43 and 50, the Roman historian, Tacitus, could already write of London as filled with negotiatores and as a place well known for its commercial prosperity. So in less than a decade it had progressed from a supply base into a flourishing town. Negotiatores are not necessarily

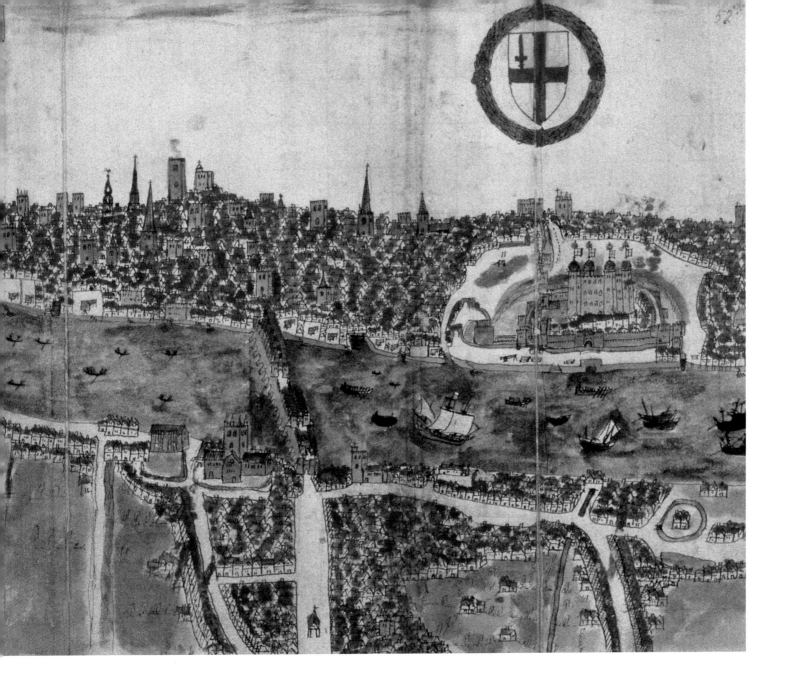

*An early
representation of
the Thames and
London Bridge.*

merchants but men of negotium; business and negotiation. They can be described as traders and brokers. Thus the line of continuity – it might almost be called the line of harmony – can still be traced. The shining buildings which now stand upon the Roman wall contain brokers and dealers who are the descendants, direct or indirect, of those who came to London in the first century. The City has always been established upon the imperatives of money and of trade.

London is based upon power: it is a place of execution and oppression, where the poor have always outnumbered the rich. Many terrible judgements of fire and death have visited it. Barely a decade after its foundation a great fire of London utterly destroyed its buildings. In AD 60 Boudicca and her tribal army laid waste the city with flame and sword, wreaking vengeance upon those who were trying to sell the women and children of the Iceni as slaves. It is the first token of the city's appetite for human lives. The evidence of Boudicca's destruction is to be found in a red level of oxidised iron among a layer of burnt clay, wood and ash. Red is London's colour, a sign of fire and devastation.

Immediately after the Boudiccan assault the work of rebuilding was begun. If you were to stand now at the great crossroads in the City, where Gracechurch Street divides Lombard Street from Fenchurch Street, you would be facing the main entrance of the Romans' public forum, with shops and stalls and workshops on either side.

The influence of Roman civilisation was enduring. The chief cashier's office in the eighteenth-century Bank of England was based upon the design of a Roman temple, very like the basilica situated to the left of the early forum. Throughout the centuries London has been celebrated or denounced as a new Rome – corrupt or mighty, according to taste – and it can safely be said that part of its identity was created by its first builders.

London began to grow and flourish. A greater forum, and a greater basilica, were built upon the same site in the late first century; the basilica itself was larger than St Paul's. A great fort was built to the north-west, where the Barbican now stands. There were public baths, and temples, and shops, and stalls; there was an amphitheatre where the Guildhall now rests, and just south of St Paul's a racing arena.

We can cite many of the ancient streets – Milk Street, Wood Street, Aldermanbury among them – as the visible remnants of a Roman street horizon. It is suggestive, also, that the great markets of London at Cheapside and East Cheap lay until recent years on the thoroughfares established by the Romans on their first arrival. In the space of fifty years, by the end of the first century, London had acquired its destiny. It became the administrative and political capital of the country as well as its trading centre. The focus of communication and commercial activity, it was governed by imperial laws concerning trade, marriage and defence, laws that survived the passing of the Romans themselves. It was in all essentials a city-state with its own independent government, albeit in direct relationship to Rome; that independence, and autonomy, will be found to mark much of its subsequent history.

Yet the security and prosperity of London are not at this early date so certain. Like an organic being London grew and developed outwards, always seeking to incorporate new territory, but it also suffered periods of weariness and enervation when the spirit of the place hid its head. We may find tokens of just such a change by those same eastern banks of the Walbrook. Here was discovered, in 1954, the remains of a temple devoted to Mithras and

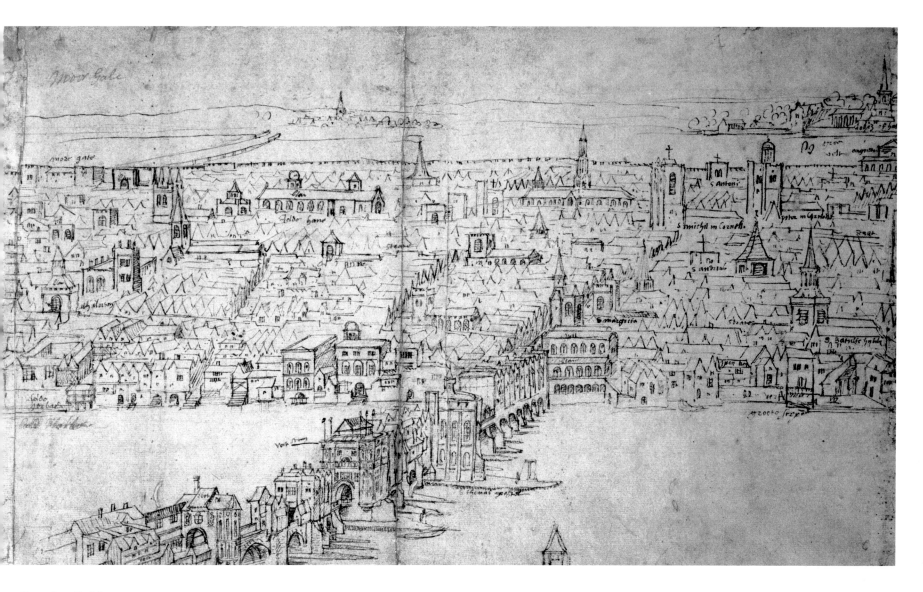

London Bridge, drawn by Anthonis van den Wyngaerde in the middle of the sixteenth century.

subsequently to other pagan deities. The Mithraic mystery cult, with its rites of initiation and the secrets of its arcane ritual, seems to presage a more disturbed and anxious city.

The most resourceful period of Roman London lay in the years spanning the first and second centuries, but these were followed by an uneven period combining development and decline. That decline was in part associated with the two great titular spirits of London, fire and plague, but there was also a steady alteration of imperial rule as the empire itself weakened and decayed. In approximately AD 200, some fifty years before the temple of Mithras was erected, the great wall was constructed around London. It speaks of an age of anxiety, but the very fact of its erection suggests that the city still had formidable resources of its own. The first London mint was established in the third century, testifying once again to the city's true nature. In that century, too, a riverine wall was constructed to complete the city's defences.

In 410 Rome withdrew its protecting hand. There are reports of raids against the city by Angles and Saxons, but there is no record of any great collapse or transition.

An Anglo-Saxon map of Britain, which has here taken on a spiritual shape. The main source of continuity lay within the Christian Church.

The arrival of the Saxons has been dated to the beginning of the fifth century when, according to the historian Gildas, the land of Britain was licked by a 'red and savage tongue'. Within certain cities 'in the midst of the streets lay the tops of lofty towers, tumbled to the ground, stones of high walls, holy altars, fragments of human bodies'. But in fact the Angles and the Saxons were already living in the London region, and it is clear from the archaeological evidence that by the late fourth century troops of Germanic origin were guarding London as legionnaires under the imperial banner.

It was once assumed, however, that the arrival of the Saxons resulted in the destruction and desertion of the city itself. In fact there was no fiery carnage in the London area from which Rome retreated. On several sites has been found a layer of 'dark earth' which was believed to indicate dereliction and decay, but contemporary experts have suggested that levels of dark soil may point to occupation rather than destruction. There is other evidence of the continuous habitation of London during that period once known as the 'dark ages'. In one of those extraordinary instances of historical survival, it has been shown that the provisions of London law in the Roman period – particularly in terms of testamentary provisions and property rights – were still being applied throughout the medieval period. There was, in other words, a continuous administrative tradition which no Saxon occupation had interrupted.

The old chronicles assert that London remained the principal city and stronghold of the Britons. In the histories of Nennius and Gildas, Geoffrey of Monmouth and Bede, it is regularly cited as an independent town which is also the home of the British kings; it is the place where sovereigns were made and acclaimed, and it is the site where the citizens were called together in public assembly. It is also the chief place of defence when, on various occasions, the Britons fled within the safety of the walls. It is the seat of the British and Roman nobility, as well as representing one of the great sees of the Christian realm.

Yet in these early chronicles the distance between factual interpretation and fanciful reconstruction is short. In these accounts, for example, Merlin makes many prophecies concerning the future of the city. Another great figure who exists somewhere within the interstices of myth and history is also to be found in London: King Arthur. According to Matthew of Westminster, Arthur was crowned by the archbishop of London. Layamon adds that he entered London after his investiture. In Malory's great prose epic, derived from several original sources, known as Le Morte d'Arthur, there are many references to London as the principal city of the realm.

The less controversial documents of historians and chroniclers add detail to this picture of legendary munificence. Ecclesiastical records reveal that a synod was held, either in London or Verulamium, in 429. Some twelve years later, according to a contemporaneous chronicle, the provinces of Britain accepted Saxon domination. Although that source is silent on the fate of London, it seems to have retained its independence as a city-state. By the middle of the sixth century, however, the city can be assumed to have accepted Saxon rule. Large parts of the walled area were employed as pasture, and the great public buildings were no doubt used as marketplaces, or stockades for cattle, or as open spaces for the wooden houses and shops of a population living among the monumental ruins of what was already a distant age.

We can infer, in turn, the lineaments of Saxon London. A cathedral church was built here, and the palace of the king was maintained on a site now claimed by Wood Street and Aldermanbury. Seventh-century records mention a 'king's hall' in London, and two centuries later it was still known as 'that illustrious place and royal city'; the location of the royal palace beside the old Roman fort in the north-west of the city suggests that its fortifications had also been maintained. But there is even more striking evidence of continuity. One of the most important archaeological discoveries of recent years has been that of a Roman amphitheatre upon the site of the present Guildhall; this is exactly the location where the Saxons were known to hold their folkmoots, in an area always specified as being to the north-east of the cathedral. It seems certain, therefore, that the Saxon citizens used the ancient Roman amphitheatre for their own deliberations. It seems very likely, in turn, that the great walled city was known as the centre of authority and of power.

This would help to explain the location of the thriving Saxon town, Lundenwic – wic meaning 'marketplace' – in the area now known as Covent Garden. A typical Saxon community, in other words, had grown up just beyond the walls of the powerful city.

We may imagine several hundred people, living and working in an area from Covent Garden to the Thames. Their kilns and pottery have lately been found, together with dress pins and glass beakers, combs, stone tools and weights for their looms. All the evidence suggests that a flourishing commercial area was, therefore, surrounded by small settlements of farmers and labourers. The names and sites of Saxon villages are still to be heard within the districts of a much greater London, Kensington, Paddington, Islington, Fulham, Lambeth and Stepney among them. The very shape and irregular street line of Park Lane are determined by the old acre strips of the Saxon farmers.

Bede had said that 'Londuniu' was the capital of the East Saxons, but over the period of middle Saxon rule the city seems to have accepted the authority of any king who was

A self-portrait of the Venerable Bede, working in his scriptorium.

dominant within the region – among them kings of Kent, Wessex and Mercia. It might almost be regarded as the commercial reward for any successful leader, together with the fact that the walled city was also the traditional seat of authority. Given this changing pattern of sovereignty, however, it is not perhaps surprising that the main source of continuity lay within the Christian Church. In 601, four years after the arrival of Augustine, Pope Gregory proclaimed London to be the principal bishopric in all Britain; three years later Ethelbert of Kent erected the cathedral church of St Paul's. There follows a bare chronicle of ecclesiastical administration. In the year when St Paul's was erected Augustine, Archbishop of Britain, consecrated Mellitus as bishop of London; the citizens then formally became Christian.

And then came the Danes. They had plundered Lindisfarne and Jarrow before turning their attention to the south. The Anglo-Saxon Chronicle records that in 842 there was 'great slaughter in London', a battle in which the Vikings were beaten back. Nine years later they returned and, having pillaged Canterbury, sailed up the Thames and with a fleet of 350 ships fell upon London. The city wall along the river may well have been already in ruinous condition but, even if the Saxons had been able to mend it, the defences were not enough to withstand the army of invaders. London was entered and pillaged. Many of the citizens may already have fled; those who remained were put to the sword, if Viking custom was followed, and their huts or shops consigned to the flame.

The invaders returned sixteen years later. Their great army moved through Mercia and East Anglia intent upon capturing Wessex; in 872 they built a camp near London, no doubt to protect their warships along the river, and it seems likely that their purpose was to

One of the first representations of the medieval parliament at Westminster.

control London and the Thames basin in order to exact tribute from neighbouring kingdoms. Certainly they occupied the city itself, which was used as a military garrison and storage base. Here they remained for fourteen years. This was not a bare ruined city, therefore, as some have suggested, but once more a busy centre of administration and supply. The Norse commander, Halfdere, minted his own silver coinage which, interestingly enough, is based upon Roman originals. The tradition of literal money-making in London had been preserved since that distant period, testifying once again to the organic continuity of its financial life. Coins were minted in London for Alfred, in his role as client king of Wessex.

Then, in 883, Alfred engaged in some form of siege, mustering an English army outside the walls of the city. London was the great prize, and three years later Alfred obtained it. It was, in fact, in the city itself that his sovereignty over the whole region was formally advertised. Alfred initiated a scheme of resettlement and fortification. The walls were restored, the quays rebuilt, and all the activities of Lundenwic brought within the defences of the revived city; it is at this point that Lundenwic passes into history as Aldwych, or 'old market-town'.

London had once more become new, since Alfred instituted a scheme of works which might qualify as an early attempt at city planning. He built a road, just within the walls, from Aldgate to Ludgate; the outline of it still exists in the streets of the modern City. The alignments of new streets were plotted close to the wharves of Queenhithe and Billingsgate. He re-established London and rendered it habitable.

The early tenth century was a period of peace but in 961 there was a great fire, succeeded by an outbreak of plague fever. The cathedral church of St Paul's was destroyed in the conflagration, and once more we witness the periodic fate and fatality of the city. The succeeding years were marked by a series of Viking attacks upon the prosperous city. In 994 the Danes sent a force of ninety-five ships into the Thames in order to blockade and assault the city, but they were driven back by London's army.

Edward the Confessor left a memorial more enduring than his family's fortunes; he retired to a palace, and established a monastery, in Westminster. There had been a church there since the second century, but London antiquarians have suggested that there was once a pagan shrine to Apollo on the same site. Certainly a Roman sarcophagus, and a section of floor mosaic, have been found in the immediate vicinity. It was an area of great importance, in any case, since Westminster marked the spot where the road from Dover was united with Watling Street, which proceeded northward. At low tide it was possible to cross the river here, and to ride along the great Roman ways. Yet topography is not simply a matter of road alignments. As we have seen, Tothill Fields beside Westminster was part of a ritualised area of power and worship; a document of 785 describes it as 'that terrible place which is known as Westminster', 'terrible', in this context, meaning sacred or holy terror.

It is not inappropriate, therefore, that the founding of Westminster Abbey is enwrapped in dreams and visions. The night before the hallowing of the first Saxon church here, in the seventh century, St Peter himself appeared to a fisherman and was ferried across the river from Lambeth; the venerable figure crossed the threshold of the new church and all at once it was illuminated by a light brighter than a thousand candles. So began the history of the church of St Peter. Edward the Confessor was in turn granted a dream, or vision, which persuaded him to build a great abbey. It became the repository of sand from Mount Sinai and earth from Calvary, a beam from the holy manger of Jesus and pieces of his cross, blood from Christ's side and milk from the Virgin Mary, a finger from St Paul and hair from St Peter. Almost a thousand years later, in this place, William Blake was granted a vision of monks chanting and proceeding down the central aisle. A century before the poet's sighting, Edward the Confessor also reappeared: a chorister came upon the broken coffin of the venerable king and drew from it a skull. So the sainted king had turned into a death's head. It is perhaps an appropriate story for an abbey which has become London's city of the dead, where the generations of kings and leaders and poets lie in silent communion as a token of that great mystery where past and present are mingled together. It is the mystery, and history, of London.

In the last month of 1066, William, Duke of Normandy, marched down St Giles High Street before turning south to Westminster. He had already savaged Southwark and now intended to lay siege to London Wall by Ludgate, which was then the principal entrance to

the city. It was commonly said at the time that London 'neither fears enemies nor dreads being taken by storm' because of its defences but, in fact, after some form of secret treaty or negotiations, certain Saxon nobles opened the gate. William's troops made their way to St Paul's and Cheapside but then 'in platea urbis' – an open space or wide street – they were attacked by a group, or perhaps even an army, of citizens who refused to countenance the entry of the foreign leader.

After a great fire in 1077 which, like its predecessors, seems to have devastated much of the city, a stone tower was built. It was called the White Tower, and rose some ninety feet in the air to emphasise its power over the city. William had recognised the one central fact – that this city was the key both to his own fortunes and to those of the country he had conquered. That is why he inaugurated the transition of London from the status of an independent city-state to that nation's capital. At the same time the Norman king and his successors initiated an inspired plan of public works in order to emphasise the central place of London in the new politics. The cathedral of St Paul was rebuilt and William's successor, his son William Rufus, began the construction of Westminster Hall; a number of monastic houses and nunneries, together with priories and hospitals, were also erected in this period so that London and its environs were the site of prolonged and continual construction. The building and rebuilding have been maintained ever since. The area around the Roman amphitheatre, for example, was cleared in the early twelfth century. In the same area the first guildhall was completed by 1127, and a second built in the early fifteenth century.

The murder of Thomas à Becket in the winter of 1170 at Canterbury, ought to have been a matter for Londoners. The archbishop was known to his contemporaries as 'Thomas of London' and for many centuries he was the only Londoner to be canonised; his theatricality and flamboyance were also characteristic of the city. But there is no evidence of any popular support for his cause among Londoners. Perhaps he is one of those striking figures in the city's history who move beyond their immediate context into eternity.

Yet it was Becket's own twelfth-century biographer, William Fitz-Stephen, who celebrated the more earthly values of the city in that period. His account constitutes the first general description of London. He describes the sound or 'clatter' of the mills, turned by streams in the meadows of Finsbury and Moorgate, as well as the shouts and cries of the market vendors. There were many wine shops close by the Thames, to accommodate the local artisans as well as traders who came to the docks; there was also a large 'public eating-house', where servants could purchase bread and meat for their masters or where the local vendors

The murder of Thomas à Becket in Canterbury Cathedral on 29 December 1170. He was one of the patron saints of London.

could sit and eat. Fitz-Stephen also depicts the 'high and thick wall' which surrounded and protected all this activity, with its seven double gates and northern towers; there was also a great fortress to the east, 'the mortar used in the building being tempered with the blood of beasts', and two 'strongly fortified' castles on the western side. Beyond the walls were gardens and vineyards, the mansions of the noble and the powerful interspersed among them. These great houses were generally in the western suburbs, where Holborn is now situated, while to the north were meadows and pastures which bordered upon 'an immense forest' of which Hampstead and Highgate are the only remnants. Just beyond the city wall, on the north-western side, was a 'smooth-field' now known as Smithfield, where horses were sold every Friday. In paddocks close by, oxen and pigs were also slaughtered and sold. The same activity had taken place in precisely the same area for almost a thousand years.

A jousting tournament in London, from Froissart's fourteenth century chronicles.

Fitz-Stephen's account is distinctive for the emphasis he lays upon the energy, combativeness and vivacity of the citizens. There were games of football every evening in the fields outside the city, when the young men were watched and cheered by their teachers, parents or fellow apprentices; upon each Sunday, at the same time, there were games of combat when they rode against one another 'with lances and shields'. Even in its sports London had a reputation as a violent city. In the coldest days of winter, when the marshland of Moorfields froze, the more sportive citizens would sit upon great blocks of ice, which were pulled along by their friends; others fashioned skates from the shin bones of animals. But again there was an element of competition and violence in their pursuit; they skated towards each other until 'either one or both of them fall, not without some bodily hurt' and 'very frequently the leg or arm of the falling party' was broken. It is a world of violence and laughter mingled with what Fitz-Stephen terms 'abundant wealth, extensive commerce, great grandeur and magnificence'. His is a portrait of a city celebrating its destiny.

It was a time, therefore, of prosperity and growth. The docks were expanding, as the waterfront was continually reclaimed and extended in order to accommodate the Flemings and the French and the Hanseatics as well as the merchants from Brabant and Rouen and Ponthieu. Most of this population was itself busily engaged in commerce: the goldsmiths of Guthrun's Lane, the butchers of East Cheap, the shoe-makers of Cordwainer Street, the iron-mongers of Old Jewry, all of them involved in perpetual trade.

The city was indeed a much noisier place than it is now, filled with continual cries of porters and water-bearers as well as the general uproar of wagons and bells, of blacksmiths and pewterers beating out their wares, of carpenters and coopers working alongside each other in the same small area of lanes and alleys. There was of course the smell as well as the

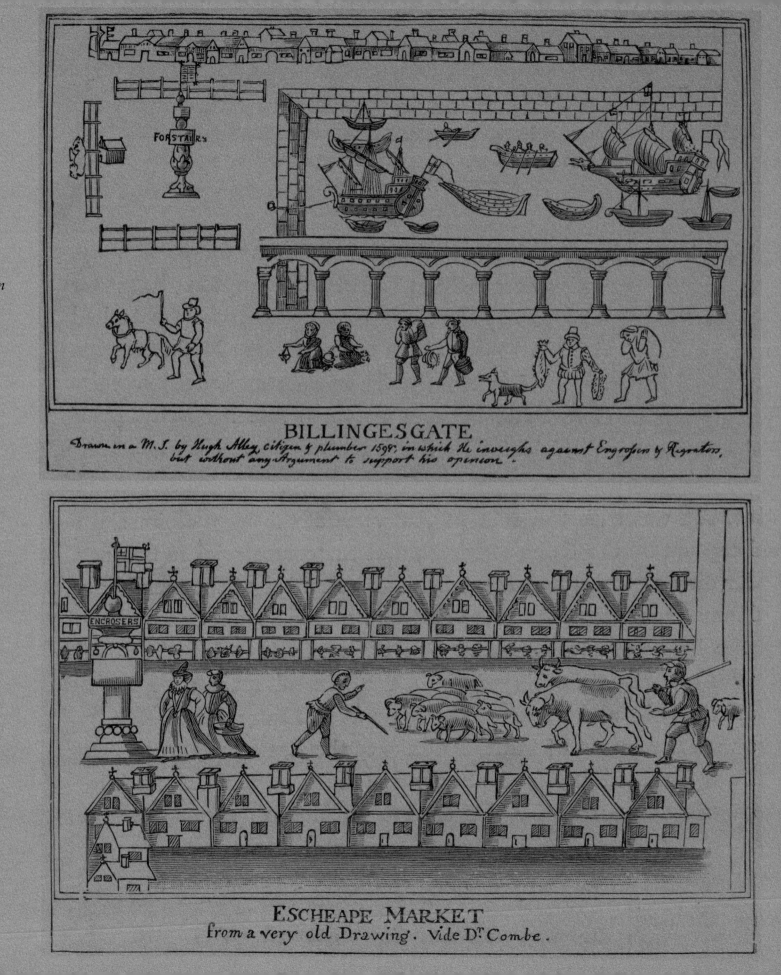

Two of London's greatest markets, in a city devoted to consumption in all of its forms.

BILLINGESGATE

Drawn in a M.S. by Hugh Alley, citizen & plumber 1598, in which He inveighs against Engrosers & Regrators, but without any Argument to support his opinion.

ESCHEAPE MARKET
from a very old Drawing. Vide Dr. Combe.

noise, concocted from tanneries and breweries, slaughter-houses and vinegar-makers, cook-houses and dung-heaps as well as the ever-flowing tide of refuse and water that ran down the middle of the narrower streets. All this created a miasma of deep odours which could not be dispersed by even the most violent wind. It was further enriched by the increased use of coal by brewers and bakers and metal-forgers.

Throughout this period, too, there was a continual process of building and rebuilding; not one part of the city was untouched by this expansion as new shops and 'sleds' or covered markets, churches and monasteries, houses of stone and timber were constructed.

There was also constant activity in the 'suburbs', or fields just outside the walls. In the twelfth century the great priories of Clerkenwell and Smithfield, St John and St Bartholomew, were established, while in the succeeding century the religious houses of Austin Friars, St Helen, St Clare and Our Lady of Bethlehem were also founded. The church of St Paul's was rebuilt, and the monastic hospital of St Mary Spital erected. Yet the grandest work in all the rebuilding was that of London Bridge. It rose in stone and became the great highway of commerce and communication which has remained upon roughly the same site for almost nine hundred years.

On either side of the southern entrance to that bridge, there now rear two griffins daubed in red and silver. They are the totems of the city, raised at all its entrances and thresholds, and are singularly appropriate. The griffin was the monster which protected gold mines and buried treasure; it has now flown out of classical mythology in order to guard the city of London. The presiding deity of this place has always been money. Thus did John Lydgate write of London in the fifteenth century: 'lacking money I might not spede'. Alexander Pope repeated his sentiments in the eighteenth, invoking, 'There, London's voice: "Get Money, Money still!"'

'The only inconveniences of London,' Fitz-Stephen wrote, 'are, the immoderate drinking of foolish persons, and the frequent fires.' In this he was prophetic as well as descriptive. A monk from Winchester, Richard of Devizes, was more colourful in his condemnation: for him London was a place of evil and wrong-doing, filled with the worst elements of every race as well as native pimps and braggarts. He referred to the crowded eating houses and taverns, where dicing and gambling were customary. It is perhaps significant that he also mentioned theatrum, 'the theatre', which suggests that the London appetite for drama was already being satisfied in forms other than those of the mystery or miracle plays staged at Clerkenwell. The monk also provided an interesting survey of the city's population, comprising in part 'pretty boys, effeminates, pederasts'. They are joined by 'quacks, belly-

Boatmen transporting passengers across the river, with Old London Bridge in the background. They were well known for their oaths and blasphemies.

dancers, sorceresses, extortioners, night-wanderers, magicians, mimes' in a panoply of urban life that would be celebrated, rather than condemned, in other centuries by writers as diverse as Johnson and Fielding, Congreve and Smollett. It is, in other words, the permanent condition of London.

William Fitz-Stephen noted that 'The city is delightful indeed, when it has a good governor'. The word itself might be construed as 'leader' or 'master', and has generally been taken to refer to the king. Yet in the years immediately succeeding his chronicle, the term is susceptible to other interpretations. There came a moment, in the last decade of the twelfth century, when it was shouted abroad that 'Londoners shall have no king but their mayor!' This short-lived revolution was the direct consequence of a king's absence on crusade in Palestine and Europe. Richard I had come to London for his coronation and was anointed on the first Sunday in September 1189 'that was marked unlucky in the calendar'; indeed it proved 'very much so to the Jews in London, who were destroyed that day'. These cryptic words describe a mass slaughter – called by Richard of Devizes a 'holocaust' – which has generally been scantily treated by historians. It has often been said that the principal culprits were those who owed money to the Jews, but it is hard to overestimate the savagery of the London mob; it represented a violent and ruthless society.

When Richard's brother, John, aspired to the crown in 1191, the citizens of London assembled at a folkmoot in order to pronounce upon his claims; at this significant moment they agreed to accept him as king as long as he in turn recognised the inalienable right of London to form its own commune as a self-governing and self-elected city-state. To this John agreed. The connotations of the word 'commune' are, from the French example, generally considered to be radical or revolutionary, but this particular revolution was instigated by the richest and most powerful of the London citizens. The honour of becoming the first mayor of London goes to Henry Fitz-Ailwin of Londenstone, who remained in office for twenty-five years until his death in 1212.

We may walk the streets of London during the long reign of Henry III (1216-72). There were great houses as well as hovels, fine stone churches against which were erected wooden stalls for passing trade. The contrast of fair and foul can be put in another context with the statistic that, out of forty thousand citizens, more than two thousand were forced to beg for alms.

The condition of the streets can be ascertained from the extant documents of the period. In the pleas and memoranda of the Guildhall, for example, we read of the master of Ludgate putting dung into the Fleet to such an extent that the water was stopped in certain places; a common privy is 'diffectif' and 'the ordur therof rotith the stone wallys'. There were complaints about defective paving in Hosier Lane, while in Foster Lane the fourteen households had the habit of casting from their windows 'ordure & vrine, the which annoyet alle the pepol of the warde'.

In the Liber Albus there are also instructions that pigs and dogs be not allowed to wander through the city; more curiously, perhaps, it was decreed that 'barbers shall not place blood in their windows'. No citizen was allowed to carry a bow for firing stones, and no 'courtesans' were permitted to dwell within the city walls. This last ordinance was persistently flouted.

It is indicative of the close watch kept upon all citizens that there were also regulations about private and social arrangements. The curfew was rung at nine o'clock in the summer months, earlier in the darkness of winter. When the bell of St Mary-le-Bow in Cheapside rang curfew, followed by the bell of St Martin's, St Laurence's and St Bride's, the taverns were cleared, the apprentices left their work, the lights dimmed as rush or candle were put out, the gates of the city were locked and bolted.

The silence was sometimes punctuated by screams, shouts and cries. It was the citizens' duty to 'raise hue and cry' against any transgressor of the peace and any citizen 'who comes not on such hue and cry raised' was heavily fined. London was a city where everyone was watching everyone else, for the sake of the spirit of the commune, and there are numerous reports of neighbours 'crying shame' at the ill treatment of an apprentice or the abuse of a wife.

It is in the context of this thriving, colourful and energetic city that we can trace specific events which reveal the dangerous condition of the streets. In court records of the period we read of unnamed beggar women collapsing and dying in the street, of occasional suicides and constant fatal accidents – 'drowned in a ditch outside Aldersgate ... fell into a tub of hot mash'. Drunkenness was general, and there are continual references to citizens falling from their solars to the ground, falling down steps into the Thames, falling off ladders. There were continual fights in the street, ambushes and arguments over nothing – or over 'goat's wool' as it was known. Games of 'dice' or 'tables' frequently ended in drunken fights, while it is clear that some of the owners of dicing taverns were engaged in wholesale fraud.

The crimes could be egregious, but the punishments had a distinctively communal aspect. The civic spirit could be violent indeed, at least when it was threatened, and there are many records of hanging or beheading for offences against the city's peace. The heads of rebels and traitors were boiled and placed upon London Bridge, sometimes adorned with a crown of ivy as a final theatrical touch in the drama of punishment. If a woman was found to be a prostitute 'let her be taken from the prison unto Aldgate' while wearing a hood of striped cloth and carrying a white taper in her hand; the minstrels once more led her to the pillory and, after the ritual abuse, she was marched down Cheapside and through Newgate to take up guarded lodgings in Cock Lane by West Smithfield. When one priest was found in flagrante delicto he was paraded through the streets with his breeches down and his clerical robes carried before him.

The visitation of the Black Death in the last months of 1348 killed around 50,000 people (about 40 per cent of London's population). A decade later, one-third of the land within the walls remained uninhabited. It was called 'the great pestilence' as well as 'the death', and reoccurred with extraordinary virulence eleven years later. London remained under the threat of bubonic plague for the rest of the century. It was transmitted by rats, living in the straw and thatch of medieval dwellings, as well as by close respiratory proximity.

Yet London seems inured to disaster, and there is no evidence of any discontinuity in the history of this period. It was said that in the city itself there were not enough living to bury the dead but, for those who survived, the disease offered an unparalleled opportunity to thrive and flourish. Many, for example, became prosperous as a result of unexpected inheritance; while, for others, the demand for labour meant that their worth was greater than they had imagined. The late fourteenth century was a time when many families, those of labourers and merchants alike, moved from the neighbouring provinces to the great city in order to make their fortunes. From this period dates the apocryphal history of Dick Whittington, which once more spread the story of London as 'Cockaigne' or the realm of gold.

In the fifteenth and sixteenth centuries epidemics of the 'sweating sickness' fell upon the capital on at least six occasions; that of 1528 'visited London with such violence that it carried off thousands in the space of five or six hours'. The quagmires and open sewers of the city turned into 'a paradise for mosquitoes', thus causing the 'ague', which is now known as malaria. No one was ever entirely well in a city 'full of pits and sloughs, very perilous and noyous', dirty and filled with 'corrupt savours'. Yet nothing could have prepared the citizens of London for the events which unfolded between the fated and fateful years of 1664 and 1666.

There is an area adjacent to Goswell Road known as Mount Mills. It is now an open space, used as a car park. It is unusual in this part of London to find what is essentially a patch of waste ground. The answer lies in its history. Here, according to Daniel Defoe in *A Journal of the Plague Year,* on 'a piece of ground beyond Goswell Street, near Mount Hill ... abundance were buried promiscuously from the Parishes of Aldersgate, Clerkenwell, and even out of the city'. It was a plague pit, in other words, where thousands were taken in 'dead carts' and dumped in the loose soil. It was comparable to the burial pit in Houndsditch, about forty feet in length, sixteen feet broad and twenty feet in depth, containing more than a thousand corpses. Some of the bodies 'were wrapped up in linen sheets, some in rags, some little other than naked, or so loose that what covering they had fell from them in the shooting out of the cart'. It was reported that the living, out of despair, sometimes flung themselves among the dead. The Pye tavern was very close to the Houndsditch pit itself, and when, at night, the drunken heard the rumble of the dead cart and the noise of the iron bell they came to the window and jeered at anyone who mourned for the newly dead. They also uttered 'blasphemous expressions' such as *There is no God* or *God is a devil.* There was one driver who 'When he had any children in his dead cart could cry "Faggots, faggots, five for sixpence" and take up a child by the leg'. The area of Mount Mills is waste ground still.

This report is taken from Defoe's chronicle. He was only six years old at the time of the visitation, and much of his evidence is anecdotal, but there are also contemporary accounts which furnish additional material for contemplation. Any observer willing to enter the city during the plague would first have noticed the silence; there was no traffic except for the dead carts, and all the shops and markets were closed. Those who had not fled had locked themselves within their houses, and the river was deserted. Any citizens who did venture

for th... ...ity of LONDON, And Parishes Adjacent:
1665. bein... ...the Account how many Persons died Weekly in every of those Years, also how many...
...Figures of the Greatness of the Calamity, and the Violence of the Distemper, in the Last Year, 1665.

John Dunstall fecit.

The Diseases and Casualties this Week.

A Rod for Run-awayes.

Gods Tokens.

Of his fearefull Iudgements, sundry wayes pronounced
upon this City, and on severall persons, both flying from it,
and staying in it.

Expressed in many dreadfull Examples of sudden Death...

By Tho. D.

Lord, have mercy ... London.

Printed at London by... ...and are to be sold at the Shop in Smithfield. 1625.

upon the streets walked in the middle, down the kennel, away from the buildings; they also avoided chance meetings. It was so quiet that the rush of water beneath the bridge could distinctly be heard throughout the old city. Great bonfires were placed at intersections and in the middle of main thoroughfares, so that the streets were filled with smoke as well as the miasma of the dead and dying. The life of London seemed to be over.

The plague had begun, in the Parish of St Giles, at the close of 1664. It is understood now that the infection was carried by the black rat, known also as *rattus rattus*, otherwise known as the ship rat or the house rat. These rats are old inhabitants of London, their bones being discovered in excavations of fourth-century Fenchurch Street. It is likely that they arrived from South Asia in Roman ships, and they have remained ever since. The severe cold of the early months of 1665 prevented any spread in the infection for a while, but from the beginning of spring the bills of mortality began to rise. By July the plague had entered the city from the western suburbs. It was a dry, hot summer without any wind. Grass grew in the abandoned streets.

Eventually the rates began to fall. In the last weeks of February 1666, there were only forty-two deaths reported, whereas more than eight thousand died each week of September 1665.

Within the texture of Defoe's prose London becomes a living and suffering being. London is itself racked with 'fever' and is 'all in tears'. Its 'face' is 'strangely altered', and its streets circulate 'steams and fumes' like the blood of those infected. It is not clear whether the whole sick body of London is an emanation of its citizens, or whether the inhabitants are an emanation or projection of the city. Certainly its conditions were responsible for much death. In the great centre of trade and commerce, the process of buying and selling itself destroyed the citizens – 'this necessity of going out of our houses to buy provisions was in a great measure the ruin of the whole city'. The people 'dropped dead in the very markets' in the act of trading. They would 'just sit down and die' with the tainted coins still in their pockets.

There is another melancholy image which issues from the pages of Defoe. It is of a city where there 'were so many prisons in the town as they were houses shut up'. Metaphors of incarceration are persistent throughout London writing, but during the Great Plague there emerged vivid and literal examples of urban imprisonment. The symbolism of the red cross and the words 'Lord have mercy on us' has not been wasted on mythographers of the city, but the measure of societal control has perhaps not been fully recognised. Of course many people escaped, often by the expedient of going over a garden wall or travelling along the roofs – even with some 'watchmen' murdered to ensure liberty – but, in theory, each street and each house became a gaol.

One ordinance has remained in force for three centuries with the proclamation that 'all the graves shall be at least six feet deep'. All beggars were expelled. Public assemblies were banned. In a city which had shown its manic propensities in a thousand different ways, order and authority had to be imposed directly and harshly. Hence the turning of houses into prisons by 'shutting up', a measure which even at the time was considered by many to be both arbitrary and pointless. But in a city of prisons it was the natural and instinctive response of the civic authorities.

red

is London's colour, a sign of fire and devastation.

Red is London's colour. The cabs of the early nineteenth century were red. The pillar boxes are red. The telephone boxes were, until recently, red. The buses are characteristically still red. The Underground trains were once generally of that colour. The tiles of Roman London were red. The original wall of London was built from red sandstone. London Bridge itself was reputed to be imbued with red, 'bespattered with the blood of little children' as part of the ancient rituals of building.

Turner's great painting 'The Burning of the House of Lords and the House of Commons, October 16, 1834'. It was the most dramatic fire of nineteenth-century London.

Red is also the colour of violence. The colour is everywhere, even in the ground of the city itself: the bright red layers of oxidised iron in the London clay identify conflagrations which took place almost two thousand years ago. Yet there is one fire which has always remained in the memory of Londoners – a fire which, as John Locke noted, created 'Sunbeams of a strange red dim light' which covered the whole of the city and could be seen even from his library in Oxford.

'The Great Fire of London' of 1666 was considered to be the greatest of fires, but in truth it was only one of a series of devastations. The fires of AD 60 and AD 125 destroyed most of the city, for example, creating what is described by archaeologists as a 'fire destruction horizon'. This is the horizon of the city itself. London burned in 764, 798, 852, 893, 961, 982, 1077, 1087, 1093, 1132, 1136, 1203, 1212, 1220 and 1227.

London seems to invite fire and destruction, from the attacks of Boudicca to those of the IRA. In the literature of the subject, there are references to particularly incandescent areas. Arthur Hardwick's Memorable Fires in London revealed Watling Street to be 'the region in the heart of the City [that] has always been a "fiery" one'. The area of St Mary Axe was destroyed in 1811, 1883, 1940 and then again in 1993. It is significant, too, that, in the city of spectacle, theatres continually go up in flame; thirty-seven were destroyed in 130 years, from 1789 to 1919, providing an appropriately theatrical scene for those who flocked to watch them. London Bridge has been destroyed by fire, as have the Royal Exchange, the Guildhall and the Houses of Parliament. In the nine years from 1833 to 1841 there were 5,000 fires in the city 'yielding an average of 556 per annum, or about three in two days'. In the 'Great London region' occurred 46,000 'primary' and 'secondary' fires.

The Great Fire, one of the most formative events of the city's history, may be dated from 1 September 1666. That evening Samuel and Elizabeth Pepys returned to their house in Seething Lane where, at three on the following morning, they were roused by a maid with news of a fire in the city. Pepys saw some flames at the lower end of a neighbouring street, and then went back to sleep. The fire had started one hour before at the house of the king's baker, Mr Farryner, in Pudding Lane. At the later enquiry Farryner insisted that before retiring to bed he had 'gone through every room, and found no fire but in one chimney, where the room was paved with bricks, which fire he diligently raked up in embers'. The cause of the Great Fire was never discovered. It just happened.

The month of August had been unusually hot, so that the thatch and timber of the neighbouring buildings in the narrow streets and alleys were already 'half-burned'. The fire found friendly territory, in other words, and was further aided by a strong south-east wind; it was carried onward from Pudding Lane towards Fish Street and London Bridge, then down through Thames Street into Old Swan Lane, St Lawrence Lane, and Dowgate. Everyone in a position to do so took to the water with boats, lighters and skiffs carrying the goods of their houses threatened by the flames. Pepys also took to the river, where with his face in the wind he was 'almost burned with a shower of fire drops'. He noticed that the 'poor pigeons were loth to leave their houses, but hovered about the windows and balconies till they burned their wings and fell down'.

The fire was now out of control, burning steadily to the north and to the west; Pepys eventually took refuge from the incendiary river in an alehouse on the other bank, and there 'saw the fire grow . . . in corners, and upon steeples, and between churches and houses, as far as we could see up the hill of the City, in a most horrid, malicious bloody flame, not like the fire flame of an ordinary fire'. It was then that he noticed the arch or bow of flame, about a mile in width.

That night the fire spread from Cheapside down to the Thames, along Cornhill, Tower Street, Fenchurch Street, Gracechurch Street and to Baynard's Castle. It had gone so far down Cheapside that it took hold of St Paul's which, by chance, was surrounded by wooden scaffolding. John Evelyn, who walked among the streets even at this hour, noted that 'the noise and cracking and thunder of the impetuous flames, the shrieking of women and children, the hurry of people, the fall of towers, houses, and churches, was like an hideous storm, and the air all about so hot and inflamed that at last one was not able to approach it'. The unprepared citizens were left bewildered; they made no attempt to put out the fires, and simply fled. Those who remained, of the 'lower' sort, stole whatever they could take from the burning dwellings. Those who did not take refuge upon the river, itself now choked with smoke and deluged by 'fire drops', went into the surrounding fields of Islington, Finsbury and Highgate, watched and wept.

By the following day, Monday, the fire had spread down Ludgate into Fleet Street and had burned down the Old Bailey; Newgate and Billingsgate were gone, while the molten lead from the roof of St Paul's ran through the streets 'glowing with fiery redness, so as no horse or man was able to tread on them'. By now the smoke stretched for fifty miles, so that those leaving the city could travel for hours in its shadow. That night several fires met together. One came down Cornhill, and one down Threadneedle Street; which, uniting together, in turn met two separate fires coming from Walbrook and Bucklersbury. John Evelyn remarked that 'all these four, journeying together, break into one great flame at the corner of Cheapside, with such a dazzling light and burning heat, and roaring noise by the fall of so many houses together, that was very amazing'. It was as if some ancient spirit of fire had reared its head in the very middle of the city.

By Tuesday the wind had abated, and the fire stopped at the top of Fetter Lane in Holborn. The deeds of the Mitre Tavern, at the other end of Fetter Lane, described a boundary by 'the tree where the Fire of London divides'. The fire was still raging in the north at Cripplegate and in the east by the Tower but the authorities, advised by Charles II, were able to stop its growth by blowing up with gunpowder houses in its path.

On Thursday John Evelyn once more walked the streets of his city, now a ruin. He found himself 'clambering over heaps of yet smoking rubbish, and frequently mistaking where I was'. This was also the experience of Londoners after the bombing raids of 1940; their city was suddenly unknown and unrecognisable. It had become an alien place, as if they had woken from some dream to encounter a quite different reality. 'Nor could anyone have possibly known where he was,' wrote Evelyn, 'but by the ruins of some church or hall that had some remarkable tower or pinnacle remaining.' The ground under his feet was so hot that he could hardly walk; the iron gates and bars of the prisons had all melted; the stones of the buildings were all calcined and rendered a brilliant white; the water left in fountains

These Engins,(which are ... the best)to qunch great Fires; are

IOHN KEELING

Made by John Keeling in Black Fryers (after many years Experience)Who also maketh all other sorts of Enguns

was still boiling while 'subterranean cellars, wells and dungeons' were belching forth 'dark clouds of smoke'. Five-sixths of the city were thus consumed, the area of devastation encompassing a mile and a half in length and half a mile in breadth. Fifteen of the city's twenty-six wards were thoroughly destroyed and, in total, 460 streets containing 13,200 houses were razed. Eighty-nine churches had gone, and four of the seven city gates were reduced to ashes and powder. It was officially reported that only six people were killed, one a watch-maker in Shoe Lane where on excavation 'his bones, with his keys, were found'.

Perhaps the most notable image of this extraordinary fire was that from a clergyman, the Revd T. Vincent, in a book entitled *God's Terrible Advice to the City by Plague and Fire*. He too had seen 'the dreadful bow' of light across the city. He had witnessed the burning of the Guildhall 'which stood the whole body of it together in view for several hours together after the fire had taken it, without flames, (I suppose because the timber was such solid oak), in a bright shining coal, as if it had been a palace of gold, or a great building of burnished brass'.

There were many representations of the events of those five days of fire, not least a series of long poems which can be found in an anthology entitled *London in Flames, London in Glory*. The burning city is severally compared to Rome, to Carthage, to Sodom and to Troy; the classical gods are depicted as wandering through the burning streets, together with Virgil and Jezebel, as the spectacle of flaming London conjures up images of dead or dying civilisations in past ages of the world. The painted images of the Fire were equally ostenta-

tious, although some of them seem literally to have been sketched at the very time of the blaze itself. There are sober studies, including those of Hollar showing 'A True and Exact Prospect of the Famous Citty of London' before the autumn of 1666 together with the same 'As It Appeareth Now After the Sad Calamitie And Destruction by Fire'; it was sketched from the south bank of the river, and it is possible to see through the ruins right into Cheapside itself. But most works were in the style of 'conflagration painting', according to London in Paint, which found their inspiration in 'Biblical or mythic city fires'. Two of the most famous paintings, 'after Jan Groffier the Elder', depict the towers and portcullis of Ludgate in flames as if it were the entrance to Hell itself.

There are many small scenes and episodes reflected in these paintings: the woman running with wild face and arms outstretched from the encroaching fire, the man carrying a bundle of silver plate upon his head, the carts and horses being driven in a great crowd towards the open fields. But the most striking image is that of a man carrying a child on his shoulders against a backdrop of flame; it was re-employed by Blake, Doré, and other artists as a true representation of the mysteries and sufferings of London.

But the conflation of the city and fire goes very deep indeed. By the mid-nineteenth century the sky above London was notable for 'the glowing atmosphere that hangs over the capital for miles'; the brick kilns on the perimeter of the city in that period created a ring as if of stage fire, while the great dust mountains inside the capital had the appearance of volcanoes. It was a city 'where fires can scarcely be kept under' while, in twentieth-century terms, it is characterised as an 'urban heat island'. London was popularly known as the 'Great Oven' and, in the 1920s, V.S. Pritchett confessed to the sensation of being 'smoked and kippered' in the depths of the city.

In 1666 many of the citizens immediately returned to the smoking ruins, in order to discover where their houses had once stood; they then laid claim to the area by erecting some kind of temporary shelter. On the very day that the fire was extinguished Charles II was informed that 'some persons are already about to erect houses againe in the Citty of London upon their old foundations'.

Three days later the king issued a proclamation to the citizens in which he promised that rebuilding would proceed quickly but declared that no new work could begin until 'order and direction' had been introduced. He then went on to formulate certain principles, the chief of which was that all new dwellings were to be built of brick or stone. Certain streets, such as Cheapside and Cornhill, were to 'be of such breadth as may with God's

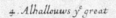

Guildhall   4. Alhallouws ye great   S. Lorentz Poultney   S. Michaels

the Royal Exchainge   S. Petris

Coke harbour   The Old Swan   Fijhmongers hall

S

A section of Wenceslaus
Hollar's panorama of
London, completed just a
few years before the Great
Fire changed the appear-
ance of the city for ever.

Southwarke

2. Gray Church

S. Dunston in the East

3. Alhallous barking

THE
BRIDGE

Lyon kay

Billings gate

blessing prevent the mischief that one side may suffer if the other be on fire, which was the case lately in Cheapside'.

Certain schemes had already been propounded, most notably by Wren and Evelyn, in which the reconstruction of London was planned upon a grand and elaborate scale. Wren proposed a series of intersecting avenues on a European model; Evelyn's new city resembled a giant chessboard dominated by twelve squares or piazzas. None was accepted, none acceptable. The city, as always, reasserted itself along its ancient topographical lines.

A committee of six was established to direct the rebuilding of the city. One of its members was Christopher Wren, who knew already that his idealised version of London was not to be achieved. A 'Fire Court' was set up to adjudicate all the claims and disputes which arose over the ownership of land and property. By February of the following year Parliament had enforced what the commission suggested. Certain streets were widened but, not surprisingly, very few alterations were made. King Street was formed, and a small thoroughfare widened into Queen Street, so that the Guildhall could be approached directly from the Thames. A more noticeable change, however, was enforced upon the size and fabric of the houses themselves. They were to be built of brick or stone, as the king had declared, and there were to be four classes or types of houses 'for better regulation, uniformity and gracefulness'. In other respects the old lines of the city were to be renewed. Within two years of the Fire twelve hundred houses had been completed, and in the following year another sixteen hundred. It was not quite the rapid and vigorous process which some historians have assumed, and for some years London had all the aspects of a ruined city, yet gradually it was rising once again.

In the aftermath of the Great Fire emerged a yellow-flowering plant known as London Rocket; it was seen again, in 1945, after the Blitz, 'just outside the City boundary'. This was not the only parallel between these two momentous events. James Pope-Hennessy, recalled that 'The city fire of December 1940 did at one moment look like Pepys' famous description of the fire of 1666. The night sky, lit by a wavering orange glare, seemed to display an aura not at all unlike his "bow of flame". And indeed, it was said by many Londoners that the 'Great Fire' had come again.

It began with attacks upon outer London. Croydon and Wimbledon were hit and, at the end of August, there was a stray raid upon the Cripplegate area. Then, at five p.m. on 7 September 1940, the German air force came in to attack London. Six hundred bombers, marshalled in great waves, dropped their explosive and high incendiary devices over east

'Among London Searchlights', a painting by C.R.W. Nevinson, dating from the Second World War.

London. Beckton, West Ham, Woolwich, Millwall, Limehouse and Rotherhithe went up in flames. Gas stations, and power stations, were hit; yet the Docks were the principal target. The firemen had to race, through fire and perpetual explosion, to reach conflagrations which were almost 'out of hand'. One volunteer, quoted in *Courage High*, a history of London fire-fighting by Sally Holloway, was on the river itself where 'half a mile of the Surrey shore was ablaze . . . burning barges were drifting everywhere . . . Inside the scene was like a lake in Hell.' In the crypt of a church in Bow 'people were kneeling and crying and praying. It was a most terrible night.'

The German bombers came back the next night, and then the next. The Strand was bombed, St Thomas's Hospital was hit together with St Paul's Cathedral, the West End, Buckingham Palace, Lambeth Palace, Piccadilly, the House of Commons. Truly to Londoners it seemed to be a war on London. Between September and November almost 30,000 bombs were dropped upon the capital. In the first thirty days of the onslaught almost six thousand people were killed, and twice as many badly injured. On the night of the full moon, 15 October, 'it seemed as if the end of the world had come'. Some compared London to a pre-historic animal, wounded and burned, which would disregard its assailants and keep moving massively onward; this was based on the intuition of London as representing some relentless and ancient force which could withstand any shock or injury. Yet other metaphors were in use – among them those of Jerusalem, Babylon and Pompeii – which lent a sense of precari-ousness and eventual doom to the city's plight. When in the first days of the Blitz Londoners saw the ranks of German bombers advancing without being hindered by anti-aircraft fire, there was an instinctive fear that they were witnessing the imminent destruction of their city.

The earliest reactions were, according to the reports of Mass Observation and other interested parties, mixed and incongruous. Some citizens were hysterical, filled with overwhelming anxiety, and there were several cases of suicide; others were angry, and stub-bornly determined to continue their ordinary lives even in the face of extraordinary dangers. Some tried to be jovial, while others became keenly interested spectators of the destruction all around them, but for many the mood was one of spirited defiance.

It is difficult fully to define that particular spirit, but it is of the utmost interest in attempting to describe the nature of London itself. In his definitive study, *London at War*, Philip Ziegler has suggested that 'Londoners made a deliberate effort to seem nonchalant and unafraid', but this self-control may have been a necessary and instinctive unwillingness to spread the contagion of panic. What if this city of eight million people were to regress into hysteria? It was precisely that fate which Bertrand Russell had predicted in a pamphlet,

Left: A German V1 flying over London.

Right: Over one hundred thousand London houses were destroyed. St Paul's survived but it rose over a blasted and wasted city.

The spirit and determination of ordinary Londoner, were unaffected by the conditions o war.

Which Way to Peace?, in which he anticipated that London would become 'one vast bedlam, the hospitals will be stormed, traffic will cease, the homeless will shriek for peace, the city will be a pandemonium'. It is possible that ordinary citizens, with instincts finer than those of their erstwhile 'betters', knew that this could not be allowed to happen. So the 'calmness, the resigned resolution of the Londoner' was the quality which impressed those coming from outside. In all of its periodic crises, and riots, and fires, London has remained surprisingly stable; it has tipped, and tilted, before righting itself. This may in part be explained by the deep and heavy presence of trade and commerce within its fabric, the pursuit of which rides over any obstacle or calamity. One of Winston Churchill's wartime phrases was 'Business as usual', and no slogan could be better adapted to the condition of London.

Yet there was another aspect of the calmness and determination of Londoners in the autumn and winter of 1940, springing from some deep sense that the city had suffered before

and had somehow survived. Of course nothing could equal the fury and destruction of the Blitz, but the sheer persistence and continuity of London through time lent an intimate yet perhaps at the time unidentifiable reassurance. There was always the intimation of eventual renewal and reconstruction. The poet Stephen Spender, in north London in the aftermath of one raid, related: 'I had the comforting sense of the sure dark immensity of London.' Here is another source of consolation; the city was too large, too complex, too momentous, to be destroyed. 'We can take it' was one of the often recorded comments by those who had been bombed out of their homes, with the unspoken addition that 'we have taken everything else'.

Henry Moore's 'Two Sleepers'. Londoners used the deep platforms of the London Underground as a refuge against the bombs.

Winston Churchill's slogan was, 'Business as usual'. It is the perfect expression of the London sensibility.

The attitude of self-sufficiency was often accompanied by an element of pride. 'Every one absolutely determined,' one observer, Humphrey Jennings, wrote, 'secretly delighted with the privilege of holding up Hitler.' There was, according to Ziegler, 'a strange lightness of heart . . . Londoners felt themselves an elite'. They were proud of their own sufferings, in the same way that earlier generations of Londoners claimed an almost proprietorial interest in their noxious fogs, in the violence of their streets, in the sheer anonymity and magnitude of their city. In a sense Londoners believed themselves to be especially chosen for calamity. This may in turn help to explain the evident fact that 'macabre exaggeration became a hallmark of many Londoners' conversation', particularly on the numbers of the dead and the wounded. The innate theatricality of London life affords one explanation; it has been said that there 'was never any conflict in the city's history to match the drama of the Second World War'. London firemen claimed that half their time was spent in dispersing crowds of interested spectators rather than fighting the conflagrations. If it were not for the sheer blank monotony of tiredness and suffering, suffused with the horror of the bombs, one might almost sense a gaiety or delight in destruction itself.

There are other images of these early months. One was of the black-out which plunged one of the most brilliantly illuminated cities of the world into all but total darkness. It became once more the city of dreadful night, and aroused in some inhabitants sensations

After the war a third of the city lay in ruins. The fatalities numbered more than thirty thousand.

of almost primitive fear as once familiar thoroughfares became lost in blackness. One of Evelyn Waugh's characters notes that 'Time might have gone back two thousand years to the time when London was a stockaded cluster of huts'; urban civilisation had been established upon light for so long that, in its absence, all customary certainties fell away. Of course there were some who took advantage of the darkness for their own purposes, but for many others the predominant sensation was one of alarm and insufficiency. The lure of shelter under the ground has already been discussed, together with the fear of administrators that London would breed a race of 'troglodytes' who would never wish to come to the surface. The reality, however, was both more stark and more prosaic. Only 4 per cent of the city's population ever used the London Underground for night shelter, largely on account of the overcrowded and often insanitary conditions which they would have found there. In implicit compliance with the tradition of London as a city of separate family dwellings, most citizens elected to stay in their own houses.

The bombings of 1940 culminated in the most celebrated and notorious of all raids,

During some great fires it seemed that the end of the world had come.

Asleep on the escalators in the Underground. As the conflict continued, Londoners grew tired and depressed. When, and how, would it end?

that of Sunday 29 December 1940. The warning was sounded a little after six in the evening, and then the incendiaries came down like 'heavy rain'. The attack was concentrated upon the City of London. The Great Fire had truly come again. The area from Aldersgate to Cannon Street, all of Cheapside and Moorgate, was in flames. One observer on the roof of the Bank of England recalled that 'the whole of London seemed alight! We were hemmed in by a wall of flame in every direction.' Nineteen churches, sixteen of them built by Christopher Wren after the first Great Fire, were destroyed; of the thirty-four guild halls, only three escaped; the whole of Paternoster Row went up in flames, destroying some five million books; the Guildhall was badly damaged; St Paul's was ringed with fire, but escaped. 'No one who saw will ever forget,' William Kent wrote in *The Lost Treasures of London*, 'their emotions on the night when London was burning and the dome seemed to ride the sea of fire.' Almost a third of the city was reduced to ash and rubble. By curious coincidence, however, the destruction was largely visited upon the historical and religious aspects of the old city; the thoroughfares of business, such as Cornhill and Lombard Street, remained relatively unscathed

The Thames some-times glowed red as if it were a river of blood. It seemed to Londoners to be a war against London itself.

while none of the great financial centres was touched. The deities of the city protected the Bank of England and the Stock Market, like the city griffins which jealously guard its treasure.

One who walked through the ruins the day after the raid recalled that 'The air felt singed. I was breathing ashes . . . The air itself, as we walked, smelt of burning.' There are many accounts of the craters, the cellars opened to the outer air, the shattered walls, the fallen masonry, the gas-mains on fire, the pavements covered with dust and broken glass, the odd stumps of brick, the broken and suspended stairs. 'For some days the church walls steamed and smoked,' according to James Pope-Hennessy in an account entitled *History Under Fire*. Yet the workers, the temporary inhabitants, of the city came back. After the raids, 'the whole city seemed to be on the tramp' as the clerks and secretaries and office boys all took circuitous ways through the ruins to their destinations. Many had arrived to find their places of employment 'gutted' or absolutely destroyed, and then returned on the following morning 'simply because they had nothing better to do'.

The city had become unfamiliar territory. The area between St Mary le Bow in Cheapside and St Paul's Cathedral reverted to wasteland, where the long grass was crossed by beaten paths bearing the names of Old Change, Friday Street, Bread Street and Watling Street. Signs were nailed up, with the names of these streets and others, to prevent people from losing their way. Even the colours of the city had changed; concrete and granite had 'been scorched umber' while church ruins were 'chrome yellow'. There are some remarkable photographs, taken by Cecil Beaton in the aftermath of the December raid. Paternoster Row is a mound of broken rubble with odd pieces of ironwork sticking out among the brick and stone; the premises of thirty publishers were destroyed. In the last Great Fire the Row was similarly struck and, according to Pepys, 'all the great booksellers almost undone'. Outside the church of St Giles, Cripplegate, the statue of Milton had been blown off its plinth by the blast of a bomb but the tower and walls of the church survived as they had done almost four hundred years before. It was recorded on 12 September 1545 that 'Sant Gylles was burned, alle hole, save the walles, stepall, and alle, and how it came God knoweth'; now, almost by a miracle, they were saved again. There are photographs of many ruined church interiors, with monuments tumbled down, screens fallen into fragments, and cherubs' heads scattered across the floor; there are photographs of the ruined Guildhall, of the bombed Middle Temple, of craters and falling roofs. It seemed to many that the tangible and textural history of London was without meaning, if its glory could disappear in a night; it was too fragile, and frail, to be relied upon. It was the invisible and intangible spirit or presence of London

A German bomber, using the Thames to chart its course.

The great parks of London were used as allotments to grow vegetables.

that survived, and somehow flourished, in the period of devastation.

There were, however, unexpected discoveries. A section of the Roman Wall, hidden for many hundreds of years, was uncovered by the bombing of Cripplegate. An underground chamber paved with tiles emerged below the altar of St Mary le Bow, and a 'Gothic blocked-up doorway' was recovered in St Vedast's, Foster Lane, after its bombardment. One contemporary has described how 'many acres of the most famous city in the world have changed from the feverish hum and activity of man into a desolate area grown over with brightly coloured flowers and mysterious with wild life'. The transformation was 'deeply affecting'. In Bread Street and Milk Street bloomed ragwort, lilies of the valley, white and mauve lilac. 'Quiet lanes lead to patches of wild flowers and undergrowth not seen in these parts since the days of Henry VIII.' The connection here with the sixteenth century is an appropriate one, when this part of London was laid out with gardens and pathways. Pigs were kept, and vegetables cultivated, in wasteland beside the bombed Cripplegate Church; this earth had been covered with buildings for more than seven centuries, and yet its natural fertility was revived. It is indirect testimony, perhaps, to the force and power of London which kept this 'fertility' at bay. The power of the city and the power of nature had fought an unequal battle, until the city was injured; then the plants, and the birds, returned.

After the great fire-raid at the end of December 1940, the attacks were more sporadic but no less deadly. There were raids in January 1941, with a brief cessation in February, but they began again in earnest in March. On 16 April the city was visited by what the Germans described as 'the greatest air-raid of all time'; the bombers returned again three nights later. More than a thousand people were killed on each night of the bombardment, which hit areas as diverse as Holborn and Chelsea. London became confused and misshapen, while anxiety and loss of sleep marked the faces of Londoners. It was the crushing sense of unreality, and meaninglessness, which now weighed heaviest; the weariness combined with the destruction to create a light-headedness among the population. 'So low did the dive-bombers come,' one witness recalled, 'that for the first time I mistook bombers for taxi-cabs.'

The heaviest and most prolonged raid of all occurred on Saturday 10 May 1941, when bombs fell in Kingsway, Smithfield, Westminster and all over the city; almost 1,500 were killed. The Law Courts and the Tower of London were attacked, the House of Commons reduced to a shell. The church of St Clement Danes was destroyed, so devastated that its rector died 'from the shock and grief' in the following month. His wife died four months later. This perhaps represents a small amount of suffering, compared to the totality of misery endured during these years, but it marks one pertinent aspect of London's

Blitz kids

The children of London were known for their endurance and fearlessness during the wartime bombings.

During the summer of 1940 one hundred thousand children were evacuated from the capital. But such was the allure of London that 2,500 came back every week.

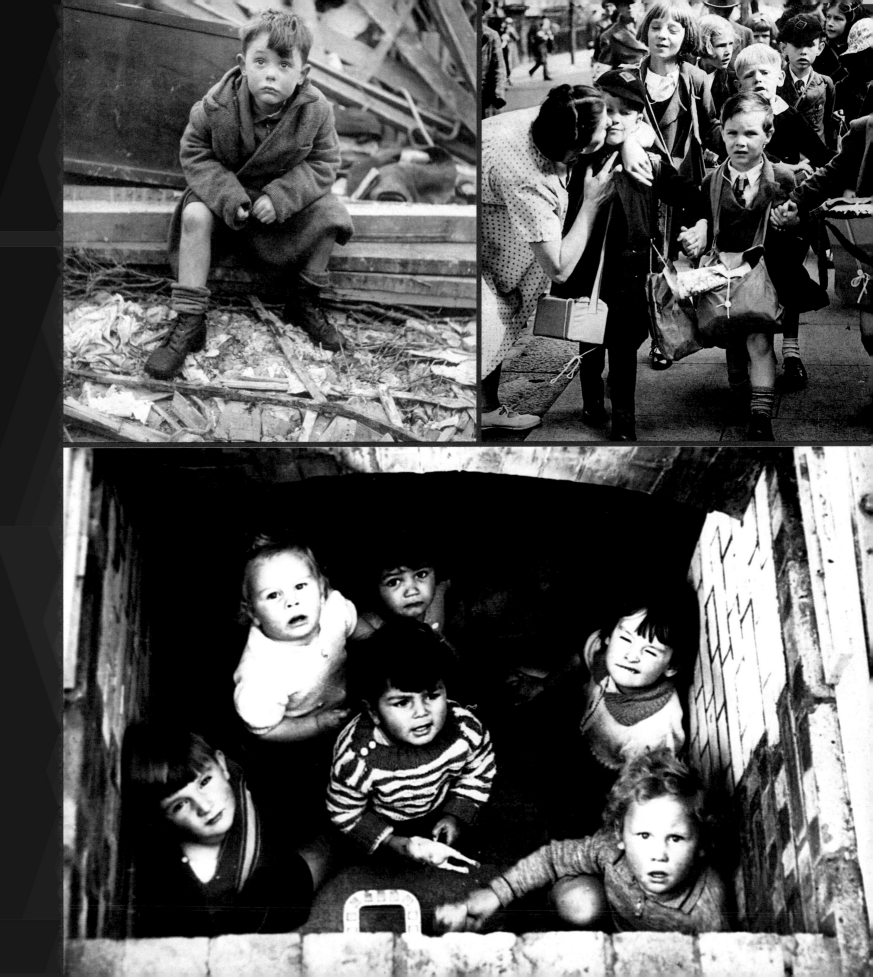

destruction; certain individuals can become so attached to, or associated with, certain buildings that their destruction provokes death itself. The city and its inhabitants are intertwined, for better or for worse. On the following day 'the smell of burning was never so pronounced as on that Sunday morning'. It seemed then that the city could not withstand the onslaught for much longer. Yet it was to be the last significant attack upon London for three years.

The German invasion of Russia had indirectly saved the city from more destruction, and there succeeded a relative peace. Then 'life' went on. The city seemed to resume its normal course, with its postmen and bus-drivers and milkmen and errand boys, but there was the strangest feeling of ennui or despondency after the spectacular damage of the Blitz. Philip Ziegler in *London at War* has described it as an 'enervating lull'. With the conflict taking place in other cities and over other skies, 'Londoners felt that they had been left on the sidelines, they were bored and dejected.' Those who still used the Underground shelters had established a network of friendship and camaraderie but this subterranean spirit was an odd token of London's general condition, in what Elizabeth Bowen called 'the lightless middle of the tunnel', enduring the discomforts and disadvantages of a war over which it had no control. The citizens were frustrated at, and bored by, the privations of life. And this in turn affected the very atmosphere and character of London itself. The people were shabbily dressed and, in instinctive and intimate sympathy, their houses became shabby. The windows were cracked, the plaster was flaking away, the wallpaper manifested signs of damp. The public buildings of the city were also showing signs of fatigue and depression, as their façades became more grimy and decayed. The atmosphere was woebegone, with a strange symbiosis between the city and its inhabitants which suggests – as Defoe had discovered during the Great Plague – the presence of a living, suffering organism.

Then, at the beginning of 1944, the bombs returned. But the 'little blitz', as it was called, was the unhappy end of unfinished business; there were fourteen raids in all, the heaviest in February and March, directed against a city which had been wearied and to a certain extent demoralised by the prolonged and uncertain conflict. 'London seems disturbed by the raids and less ebullient than in 1940-1,' Jock Colville noted. Then something else happened. In the June of that year pilotless jet planes carrying a bomb known as the V1, alias doodle-bug, alias flying bomb, alias buzz bomb, alias robot bomb, began to appear in the skies above London. They were recognised by the sharp buzzing of the engine followed by sudden silence, as the engine cut out and the bomb fell to earth. They came in daylight, with infrequent intervals between them, and were perhaps the hardest to bear. 'One listens fascinated to the Doodle Bugs passing over,' one contemporary wrote, 'holding one's breath, praying that they will travel on . . . The atmosphere in London has changed. Back into the Big Blitz. Apprehension is in the air. Buses half empty in the evening. Marked absence of people on the streets. Thousands have left, and many go early to the shelters.' The novelist Anthony Powell was on fire duty and watched the V1s travelling through the air to their unknown targets, 'with a curious shuddering jerky movement . . . a shower of sparks emitted from the tail'. He saw them as 'dragons' and 'In imagination one smelt brimstone', so that the city under threat becomes once more a place of fantasy and myth. Almost two and a half thousand flying bombs fell upon the capital within ten months – 'droning things, mercilessly making for you, thick and fast, day and night'. It was the impersonality of the weapons, often compared with giant flying insects, which compounded the fear. The intended victims themselves became depersonalised, of course, so that the condition of living in the city was the condition of being less than human.

Just as the frequency of the flying bombs began to diminish, in the early autumn of 1944, Vengeance Two – the V2 – was targeted upon the capital. For the first time in the history of warfare, a city came under attack from long-distance rockets which travelled at approximately three thousand miles per hour. No warning could be sounded; no counter-attack launched. The first one hit Chiswick and the explosion could be heard at Westminster about seven miles away. Their power was so great that 'whole streets were flattened as they landed'. Almost a thousand rockets were aimed at the capital, with a half reaching their tar-

*Churchill and other
wartime leaders on
the balcony of
Buckingham Palace
after victory.*

gets. There were open spaces where streets had been. One rocket hit Smithfield Market, and another a department store in New Cross; the Royal Hospital in Chelsea was struck. 'Are we never to be free of damage or death?' one Londoner complained. 'Surely five years is long enough for any town to have to suffer?'

It was the coldest winter for many years, and the bombs continued to fall. Illness was in the air, as it has been throughout London's troubled history, along with rumours of epidemics and mounting deaths. Yet there was also a certain insouciance abroad; the V2s were so unpredictable and random that they revived the gambling spirit of Londoners who now retired to bed without knowing if they were necessarily going to rise on the following morning.

And then, suddenly, it was all over. At the end of March 1945 a rocket fell upon Stepney, and another on Whitefield's Tabernacle on the Tottenham Court Road. But then the raids ceased; the rocket-launching sites had been captured. The skies had cleared. The Battle of London was finally won. Almost 30,000 Londoners had been killed, and more than 100,000 houses utterly destroyed; a third of the City of London had been razed.

On 8 May 1945 there were the usual celebrations for victory in Europe, VE Day, although by no means as garish or as hysterical as those of 1918. The participants were more weary, after five years of intermittent bombing and death, than their predecessors on the same streets twenty-seven years before; and the war against Japan was continuing (VJ Day was 15 August 1945). Yet something had happened to London, too. In the phrase of the period the

Victory celebrations at Piccadilly Circus.

Celebrations in Trafalgar Square.

'stuffing' had been 'knocked out of it', the metaphor suggesting a thinner and more depleted reality. Certainly it had lost much of its energy and bravura; it had become as shabby as its inhabitants and, like them, it would take time to recover.

How Shall We Rebuild London? This was the title of a book, by C.B. Purdom, published after the war. Yet even before 1945 a regional planner, Patrick Abercrombie, had prepared two proposals, the County of London Plan and the Greater London Plan, which would lend London 'order and efficiency and beauty and spaciousness' with an end to 'violent competitive passion'. It is the eternal aspiration, or delusion, that somehow the city can be forced to change its nature by getting rid of all the elements by which it had previously thrived.

Yet, in topographical terms, the Abercrombie plans were immensely influential. They required a significant shift of population within the city itself in order to 'create balanced communities each comprising several neighbourhood units'; the reconstruction of bombed London would proceed on the basis of 'density zones' which would disperse hitherto overcrowded neighbourhoods. There would be a balance of housing, industrial development and 'open space' with key highways connecting variously integrated communities. Three examples may represent many. Much of the population of Bethnal Green was rehoused in LCC 'low-density' estates such as Woodford in Essex; the bombed areas of Poplar were rebuilt as the great Lansbury Estate with a mixed style of block and single dwellings. Within inner London the Loughborough Estate rose in Brixton, its main edifices eleven storeys high. The elements of London were being redistributed, to create more light and air. The old streets, which were variously considered 'obsolete' or 'outworn', 'narrow' or 'confined', were erased in order to make room for modern, larger and neater estates.

Other elements of Abercrombie's plans were also implemented, most notably in the Town and Country Act of 1947. He proposed that London become a 'circular inland city' composed of four rings – the Inner Urban Ring, the Suburban Ring, the Green Belt Ring and the Outer Country Ring. It was a way of containing the 'inner city', as if it were some dangerous or threatening organism which could not be permitted to grow. On most maps it is painted black. It was also important to remove industry and people from this inner darkness as if the act of so doing would render it less dangerous. In order to expedite the migration of a million people another part of Abercrombie's report suggested the development of new 'satellite towns' in the Outer Country Ring. Eight of these were built, and prospered, but the effects upon London itself were not exactly as had been anticipated and planned. As any historian of London might have told the various urban boards, neither schemes nor regulations

'Slum clearance.' Hampden Crescent, off Harrow Road, 1965.

would be able to inhibit the city. It had been proposed to check its industrial and commercial growth, by siting new industries in the 'satellite towns', but London's commercial prosperity revived after war. The manufacture of cars, buses, trucks and aeroplanes rose to unprecedented levels; the Port of London handled record numbers of goods, and employed 30,000 men; the 'office economy' had restored the City of London so that it experienced a property boom. The population of the capital had dipped slightly, after the dispersal of many of its inhabitants to the suburbs and to the new towns, but the effect was mitigated by sudden and unexpectedly high fertility. Nothing could withstand the ability of the city to rejuvenate itself, and continue its growth.

The new 'satellite towns', such as Stevenage and Harlow and Basildon, became part of a historical process which was also too powerful – too instinctive – to be 'reversed'. London has always grown by taking over adjacent towns or villages and cradling them in its embrace. It has been a feature of its development since the eleventh century. And so it overtook the newly created towns. So powerful is the historical imperative that Patrick Abercrombie and his colleagues were instinctively creating just the same patterns of habitation as the seventeenth-century builders of Bloomsbury and Covent Garden. The 'new towns' ineluctably became as much part of London as their predecessors; instead of restricting the size of the city, the postwar planners immeasurably expanded it until the whole southeastern area became 'London'.

motley:

Punch, with his violence, his vulgarity and his sexual innuendo, is a recognisable urban character.

John Stow, the great sixteenth-century antiquarian, offered the most vivid and elaborate description of Tudor London. He wrote of new streets and new buildings continually springing up beyond the walls and, within the city itself, of 'encroachments on the highways, lanes, and common grounds'. Where once there had been sheds or shops, in one of which an old woman used to sell 'seeds, roots and herbs', there were now houses 'largely built on both side outward, and also upward, some three, four or five stories high'.

'Frost Fair', circa 1685. The Thames froze twenty-three times between 1620 and 1814, because the Old London Bridge impeded the movement of the water until it became sluggish.

View of London from the South Bank, showing in the foreground the Swan, the Rose and the Globe theatre

The Manor H[...] of Park Gard[...] Southwark, a [...] for gambling, [...] famous broth[...] by Elizabeth [...] Holland, kno[...] Bess, in the 1[...]

Bull- and bear-baiting on Bankside. It is possible that the bear-baiting ring and the cockpit were the models for the Elizabethan theatre.

There has been speculation about the origins of early theatre architecture, and some have supposed that it was established upon the pattern of the yards of galleried inns where itinerant groups of minstrels or actors would perform. They were known as 'inn-playhouses'; there were two in Gracechurch Street, the Bell and the Cross Keys, while another stood on Ludgate Hill. The latter was known as the Belle Sauvage or the Bell Savage and, like the others, soon acquired a distinctly unsavoury reputation. In 1580 an edict from the Privy Council commanded the officers of London 'to thrust out the Players from the City' and to 'pull down the playing and dicing houses within the Liberties' where the presence of actors encouraged 'immorality, gambling, intemperance . . . Apprentices and Factions'. The theatre, then, may provoke that unrest which seems always to have been present beneath the surface of the city's life.

Other theatrical historians have concluded that the true model of the Elizabethan theatre was not the inn-yard but the bear-baiting ring or the cockpit. Certainly these activities were not incompatible with serious drama. Some theatres became bear-rings or boxing rings, while some cockpits and bull-rings became theatres. There was no necessary distinction between these activities, and historians have suggested that acrobats, fencers and rope-dancers could also perform at the Globe or the Swan. Edward Alleyn, the great actor-manager of the early seventeenth century, was also Master of the King's Bears. The public arena was truly heterogeneous.

The popularity of Elizabethan drama characterises Londoners who attended it, both in their affection for colourful ritual and in their admiration of magniloquence. The taste of the crowd for intermittent violence was amply satisfied by the plays themselves, while the Londoners' natural pride in the history of their city was recognised in those dramatic historical pageants which were part of the diet of the playhouses. When Shakespeare places Falstaff and his company in East Cheap, he is invoking the life of the city which existed two centuries before. Spectacle and violence, civic pride and national honour, all found their natural home in the theatres of London.

During the Puritan Commonwealth the theatres were closed; it was said that the people had seen enough public tragedy and no longer required any dramatic version; instead theatrical entertainments were performed clandestinely or under cover of some other activity. The Red Bull Playhouse in Clerkenwell remained open for rope-acts and the like, but also managed to make room for 'drolleries' and 'pieces of plays'. So great was the appetite for these spectacles among ordinary Londoners that one contemporary wrote: 'I have seen the Red Bull play-house, which was a large one, so full, that as many went back for want of

The GLOBE on the Banke Side, where Shakspere acted.
From the long Antwerp view of London in the Pepysian Library.

With the drawing from which this Cut was made I was favoured by the Reverend Mr. Henley
STEEVENS.

tectum

porticus

aedilia tragica

orchestra

mimorum aedes

ingressus

proscenium

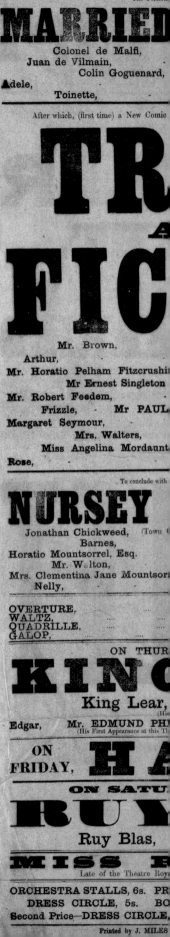

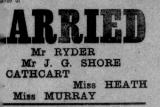

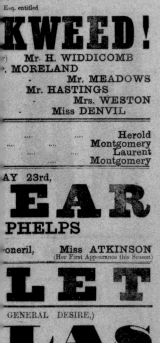

The Spanish Tragedy:

OR,

HIERONIMO is mad againe.

Containing the lamentable end of *Don Horatio*,
and *Belimperia*; With the pitifull Death
of HIERONIMO.

*Newly Corrected, Amended, and Enlarged with new
Additions, as it hath of late beene divers
times Acted.*

LONDON
Printed by *Augustine Mathewes*, for *Francis Grove*, and are to
bee sold at his Shoppe, neere the Sarazens Head,
upon Snow-hill. 1633.

10 The Roaring Girle.

OR

Moll Cut-Purse.

As it hath lately beene Acted on the Fortune-stage by
the *Prince his Players.*

Written by *T. Middleton* and *T. Dekkar.*

My case is alter'd, I must worke for my liuing.

Printed at *London* for *Thomas Archer*, and are to be sold at his
shop in Popes head-pallace, neere the Royall.
Exchange. 1611.

LEAR.   MACBETH.

RICHARD III.   HAMLET.

M.r GARRICK in Four of his Principal Tragic Characters.

149

*Grimaldi and the Alpaca
in the popular pantomime
of the 'Red Dwarf'.*

room as had entered.' There were continual complaints about plays and actors, even after various inhibitory proclamations of 1642 and 1648, so we may assume that the more spirited Londoners continued to find at least 'pieces' of drama.

It might be thought then that the citizens would agree with one of their number, Samuel Pepys, who declared after the Restoration that the theatre was 'a thousand times better and more glorious than ever before'. He was referring to the newly licensed theatres of Dorset Gardens and Drury Lane, but the new theatres were nothing like the old; as Pepys went on to remark, 'now all things civil, no rudeness anywhere'. The drama had been refined, in other words, in order that it would appeal to the king, the court and those Londoners who shared the same values. Just as the 'Cockney' dialect was now being denigrated, so the popular theatre of previous decades was dissolved.

And yet the more 'Cockney' Londoners did also manage to attend the new plays; they were not necessarily welcomed in the boxes or the pit with the more prosperous citizens, but they took over the gallery from where they could shout insults or pelt fruit upon both stage and respectable audience. Cockney theatre-goers were only one aspect, however, of the generally partisan and inflammatory aspect of the urban audience. 'Claques' would attend in order to cry up, or drown out, the latest production; fights would break out among the gentlemen 'of quality', while there were often riots which effectively concluded all theatrical proceedings. Indeed the riots themselves were somewhat theatrical in appearance. When in the mid-eighteenth century David Garrick proposed to abolish 'half-price' seats, for those who entered after the third of five acts (the whole performance beginning at six o'clock in the evening), the day appointed for that innovation found the Drury Lane Playhouse filled with a silent crowd. P.J. Grosley composed *A Tour to London* in 1772, and set the scene. As soon as the play commenced there was a 'general outcry' with 'fisty-cuffs and cudgels', which led to further violence when the audience 'tore up the benches of the pit and galleries' and 'demolished the boxes'. The lion, which had decorated the king's box, was thrown upon the stage among the actors, and the unicorn fell into the orchestra 'where it broke the great harpsichord to pieces'. In his *London Journal* of 19 January 1763, Boswell remarks that 'we sallied into the house, planted ourselves in the middle of the pit, and with oaken cudgels in our hands and shrill-sounding cat calls in our pockets, sat ready prepared'.

Such behaviour in the capital's theatres continued into the nineteenth century. A German traveller of 1827, Prince Pückler Muskau, reported that 'The most striking thing to a foreigner in English theatres is the unheard-of coarseness and brutality of the audiences.' The 'Old Price' riots of 1807 lasted for seventy nights, and the private life of Edmund Kean

A pugilistic episode in 'High Life in London'. The city has always enjoyed violence.

– accused of being both a drunk and an adulterer – led to four nights of violent rioting in the playhouse of Drury Lane. What was termed 'party spirit' did on more than one occasion prompt fights both among the spectators and the players. The presence of foreigners upon the stage was another cause of uproar; when the 'Theatre Historique' arrived at Drury Lane from Paris, there was a general rush for the stage. Mobs surrounded the Theatre Royal in the Haymarket, in 1805, when a comedy entitled *The Tailors* caused offence among the fraternity. Professional boxers were brought into the auditorium by rival groups, as early as 1743, in order to slug it out. This was city drama, in every sense. And yet, in the city itself, the real drama was still performed upon the streets.

Charles Lamb, that great Londoner, extolled his city as 'a pantomime and masquerade . . . The wonder of these sights, impels me into night-walks about her crowded streets, and I often shed tears in the motley Strand from fulness of joy at so much life.' Macaulay

Left: Meat – especially beef – was the staple of the London diet. Note the butcher in his blue costume.

Right: Colourfully costumed theatrical 'types' at a gala. Crowds, and mobs, were a feature of London life.

wondered at the 'dazzling brilliancy of London spectacles'. For these Londoners, whether by birth or adoption, the theatricality of London is its single most important characteristic.

Everyone in London wore a costume. From the earliest period the city records reveal the vivid displays of rank and hierarchy, noting garments of coloured stripes and gowns of rainbow hues. When the dignitaries of the city attended the first day of Bartholomew Fair, for example, they were expected to wear 'violet gowns, lined', but the emphasis on colour and effect was shared by all manner of London citizens. In fact in such a crowded city people could be recognised only by their costume, the butcher by his 'Blue-Sleeves and Woollen Apron' or the prostitute by 'Hood, Scarf and Top-Knot'. A shopkeeper of the mid-eighteenth century would advertise the traditional worth of his wares 'with his hair full-powdered, his silver knee and shoe buckles, and his hands surrounded with the nicely-plaited ruffle'. In the early twentieth century it was noted that the bank messengers and fishboys, waiters and city policemen, still wore mid-Victorian costume as if to display their antique deference or respectability. In any one period of London's history, in fact, it is possible to detect the presence of several decades in the dress and deportment of those in the streets.

London has always been considered to be the home of stock theatrical characters – the 'shabby genteel', the 'city slicker', the 'wide boy'. In print-shop windows of the mid-eighteenth century there were caricatures of London 'types', while the more fashionable citizens of the same period dressed up in costume for masques and disguisings. The most famous pictorial series displaying London characters and tradesmen is Marcellus Laroon's *The Cryes of the City of London Drawne after the Life*, published in 1687; it is also an anthology of

patter and street cries. An even earlier record is the medieval poem 'London Lickpenny'. We hear the merchants of Cheapside sing 'Strabery ripe' and 'Cherryes in the ryse'. 'Here is Parys thred, finest in the land . . . Hot shepe's feete . . . Makerell . . . ryshes grene!' The coster-monger sold 'Costards!', which were big apples, but in later centuries the 'coster', with his horse and cart, cried out, 'Soles, oh! . . . Live haddick . . . Ee-ee-eels alive, oh! . . . Mackareel! mack-mack-mackareel!' So it continued, down other streets and other centuries.

As London grew larger and noisier, the cries became louder – perhaps, even, more desperate and more hysterical. From a distance of half a mile, they were a low, steady and continuous roar much like a fall of water; they became a Niagara of voices. The cries of the street-seller were joined by those of the 'common criers' who announced such items of public news as 'If any man or woman can tell any tydyngs of a grey mare, with a long mane and a short tayle . . .' There were the shopkeepers of Cheapside, Paternoster Row, East Cheap and a hundred other localities calling out continually 'What do you lack . . . Will you buy . . .'. The cry of the 'mercury-women', 'London's Gazette here', was eventually superseded by that of the newsboy with his 'Pa-a-par! ainy of the mornin' pipers'. The horn of the sow-gelder plying his trade mingled with the bell of the dustman and the sound of the 'Twancking of a brass Kettle or a Frying-pan' together with the myriad and unending sounds of the London traffic.

Today, street markets are still alive with chatter and patter; most of the cries have vanished, although even in the twenty-first century you might still hear the bell of the muffin-man or the horn of the knife-grinder and see the pony-and-trap of the 'any-old-iron' or

Below: The fishmonger rides his fish, the parson a Bible, the tailor a goose and the lawyer his brief. London 'types' take advantage of a craze for hobby horses in 1819.

Right: Street criers – here selling lavender and matches – were a permanent feature of the London streets.

Right: The characters of 'Oliver Twist', penny plain or twopence coloured. Dickens turned the urban world into a pantomime.

Girls and boys come out to play

Punch and Judy, 1931.

Top right: On the first of May every year chimney-sweeps, painted as 'lily-whites', banged their brushes and climbing tools as they paraded through the city.

Right: Showmen would display toys and kites.

Bottom right: Street children were known as 'little Arabs', recalcitrant children of more affluent families as 'little radicals'.

A Transfer of Property.

This page: Acrobats made unforgettable street performers.

Opposite: A performance of Charles Dickens's fiction at the George Inn, Southwark, 1938.

rag-and-bone man. There were also the barrow man with 'Shrimps and winkles all alive-o', the lavender seller, and the 'lilywhite' celery and watercress man who cried out, ''Ere's yer salory and watercreases.'

The stages of sixteenth-century theatres were built to face the south, so that more light might fall upon the players, but we may imagine the actions and deportment of less professional actors to be similarly lit upon the crowded thoroughfares of London. Historical scenes were dramatised by street performers. There are extant photographs of actors in nineteenth-century street theatre; they seem poor, and perhaps grimy, but they wear spangling tights and elaborate costumes against garishly painted backdrops. In the early twentieth century, too, scenes from the novels of Dickens were played out on open carts on the very sites where those scenes were set.

Dickens may have appreciated such a gesture, since he turned London itself into a vast symbolic theatre; much of his dramatic imagination was formed by visiting the play-houses which abounded in his youth, particularly the penny gaffs and the small theatrical 'houses' around the Drury Lane Theatre. In *Vanity Fair* his contemporary, Thackeray, noted two London boys as having 'a taste for painting theatrical characters'. In a similar spirit almost every street of London was once the object of dramatic curiosity, from *A Chaste Maid in Cheapside* to *The Cripple of Fenchurch Street*, from *The Boss of Billingsgate* to *The Lovers of Ludgate*, from *The Devil of Dowgate* to *The Black Boy of Newgate*. These plays were generally violent and melodramatic in theme, but that is precisely why they offered a true image of teeming city life.

As long as the city has existed there have been entertainers and entertainments, from the street ventriloquists who cast their voices into their hands to the 'man with the telescope' who for twopence would allow you to look at the heavens on a summer's night. Performers

balanced on the weathercock of St Paul's steeple; there were midnight dog-shows and duels of rats; there were street jugglers and street conjurors, complete with pipes and drum; there were performing bears and performing monkeys dragged through the streets of London upon long ropes. In the late eighteenth century a pedlar exhibited a hare dancing upon a tambourine, while another entertainer displayed 'a curious mask of bees on his head and face'. There are now amusement arcades where there were once the windows of print-shops, and instead of the London Zoo there was once a 'Menagerie' in Exeter Change along the Strand where the roaring of the beasts reverberated down the thoroughfare and frightened the horses.

There have always been wonders and curiosities. John Stow recorded the minute skills of a blacksmith who exhibited a padlock, key and chain which could be fastened around the neck of a performing flea; John Evelyn reported seeing 'the Hairy Woman' whose eyebrows covered her forehead, as well as a Dutch boy who displayed the words 'Deus Meus' and 'Elohim' on each iris. In the early nineteenth century 'Siamese twins' were often

It was estimated that, in the middle of the nineteenth century, one third of London's population lived in abject misery.

Mudlarks were young scavengers; little girls sold Lucifer matches.

Crossing-sweepers were reduced to begging; and chimney-sweeps, attached to their masters at the age of seven, were often broken cripples by twelve.

exhibited, although such 'monstrous couplings' had already been shown under other names in other centuries, and in the same period was displayed the 'Anatomic Vivante' or 'Living Skeleton' who at the height of five feet seven and a half inches weighed less than six stone.

Some of the greatest London wonders and curiosities, however, are its 'characters' and eccentrics. There was 'Sir' Harry Dimsdale of Seven Dials, according to *Old and New London*, 'a poor diminutive creature, deformed and half an idiot' who hawked laces and threads at the turn of the nineteenth century; he followed the same routes, along Holborn or Oxford Street, and suffered the jeers of the children and the watermen who washed down the hackney-coach stands. He had only four or five teeth, but could bend a silver coin with them 'when he could induce anybody to trust him with one'. His favourite amusement was to torment children by pinching them or throwing them to the ground, but his chief pleasure was found in drink. He was 'helplessly drunk every evening . . . howling in the frenzy produced by his fiery draughts or uttering the low, dismal plaint caused by hunger or pain'. 'Sir' Harry was known throughout London, and there is an extant engraving of him at the age of thirty-eight; but then he, too, suddenly disappeared. His is a curious story of suffering and isolation, but one with echoes and parallels in the modern city.

Other eccentric tradesmen led more amiable lives in the street. There was the famous character Peter Stokes, the 'flying pie-man' of Holborn Hill in the early nineteenth century; as described by 'Aleph' in *London Scenes and London People*, he 'always wore a black suit, scrupulously brushed, dress coat and vest, knee breeches, stout black stockings, and shoes with steel buckles'. This tradesman, with an expression 'open and agreeable, expressive of intellect and moral excellence', would dash out of Fetter Lane on the stroke of twelve noon and run through the streets of the neighbourhood for the next four hours, dodging horses and wagons and coaches, incessantly crying 'Buy! Buy! Buy!' He too was famous throughout London, and sat to an engraver with the basket of pies balanced neatly on his right arm. There was a celebrated miser, Thomas Cook of Clerkenwell, who on his death-bed demanded his money back from the surgeon who had not cured him.

Benjamin Coates first came to public notice in 1810 when he hired the Haymarket Theatre so that he might play Romeo for one night; he appeared on stage 'in a cloak of sky-blue silk, profusely spangled, red pantaloons, a vest of white muslin, and a wig of the style of Charles II, capped by an opera hat'. Unfortunately he had a 'guttural' voice and the laughter which greeted his performance was increased by the fact that 'his nether garments, being far too tight burst in seams which could not be concealed'. He was known, ever after, as Romeo Coates and was often seen driving through the streets in a carriage manufactured in the shape of a sea shell. For sheer vigour and energy we may put him beside the engraver William Woolett who, each time he finished a new work, fired a cannon from the roof of his house in Green Street, Leicester Square.

Others Londoners became notorious through their diet. In the middle years of the seventeenth century Roger Crab of Bethnal Green subsisted on 'dock-leaves, mallows or grasse' and plain water, while in the late twentieth century Stanley Green, wearing cap and blazer, paraded in Oxford Street with a banner proclaiming 'Less Passion from Less Protein'. For twenty-five years, crowds swirled about him, almost oblivious of his presence, engaged only in their usual uproar.

Londoners have characteristically used their holidays or holy days for 'violent delights'. From the early medieval period there have been archery and jousting, bowls and football – as well as the 'hurling of Stones and Wood and Iron' – but the taste of the London crowd could also be less healthful. There were cock-fights and boar-fights, bull-baiting, bear-baiting and dog-baiting. The bears were given affectionate names, such as 'Harry Hunks' or 'Sacherson', but the treatment of them was vicious. One visitor to Bankside, in the early sev-

Civil War propaganda. The forces of Cromwell set up a series of earth-works to defend London.

enteenth century, watched the whipping of a blind bear 'which is performed by five or six men, standing circularly with whips, which they exercise upon him without any mercy, as he cannot escape from them because of the chain: he defends himself with all his force and skill, throwing down all who come within his reach and are not active enough to get out of it, and tearing the whips out of their hands and breaking them'. Bulls were baited with dogs, also, but they were sometimes maddened by having peas placed in their ears, or fireworks stuck on their backs. This was the sport of the London crowd.

The more respectable seventeenth-century citizens were not necessarily amused by these diversions. Instead there were healthful 'walks' in a number of carefully planned and plotted public areas. By the early seventeenth century Moorfields had been drained and laid out, creating 'upper walks' and 'lower walks', and a few years later Lincoln's Inn Fields were also designed for 'common walks and disports'. St James's Park was designed a little later; here, in the words of Tom Brown, a contemporary journalist, 'The green Walk afforded us varieties of discourses from persons of both sexes . . . disturbed with the noisy milk folks – crying – A Can of Milk, Ladies; A can of Red Cow's Milk, Sir'. But the true 'nature' of London is not shrubbery or parkland, but human nature. At night beneath the shade of the

trees, according to the Earl of Rochester, 'Are buggeries, rapes and incests made' while Rosamond's Pond on the south-west side of St James's Park became notorious for suicides.

In Spring Gardens were a bowling green and butts for target practice. In the New Spring Gardens, later Vauxhall Gardens, there were avenues and covered walks. Small green refreshment huts sold wine and punch, snuff and tobacco, sliced ham and quartered chicken, while ladies of doubtful morals sauntered among the trees with gold watches dangling from their necks as a token of their trade. Much of that vigour has now vanished. The parks are now characteristically restful places within the noise and uproar of London. They attract those who are unhappy or ill at ease. The idle and the vagrant sleep more easily beneath the trees, together with those who are simply exhausted by the city. London parks have often been called the 'lungs' of the city, but the sound is that of sleep. 'It being mighty hot and I weary,' Pepys wrote on 15 July 1666, 'lay down upon the grass by the canalle [in St James's Park], and slept awhile.'

Show! Show! Show! Show! Show! This was the cry of a seventeenth-century city crowd, as recorded in Ned Ward's London Spy. There were indeed many shows to be seen on the London streets, but the greatest fair of all was held at Smithfield. It was known as Bartholomew's Fair.

Smithfield itself began as a simple trading area, for cloth in one place and cattle in another, but its history has always been one of turbulence and spectacle. Great jousts and tournaments were held there in the fourteenth century; it was the ritual place for duels and ordeal by battle; it was the home of the gallows and the stake. That festive nature was also evident in less forbidding ways. Football matches and wrestling contests were commonly staged and the appropriately named Cock Lane, just beyond the open ground, was the haunt of prostitutes. Miracle plays were also part of its entertainment.

The trading market for cloth had become outmoded by the middle of the sixteenth century but 'the privileges of the fair' were still retained by the city corporation. So, instead of a three-day market, it was transformed into a fourteen-day festival which resounds through the plays and novels of succeeding centuries with the cry of 'What do you lack? What is it you buy?' From the beginning of its fame there were puppet-shows and street performers, human freaks and games of dice and thimble, canvas tents for dancing or for drinking, eating-houses which specialised in roast pork.

This was the fair which Ben Jonson celebrated in his play of the same name. He notes the sound of rattles, drums and fiddles. Here on the wooden stalls were laid out mousetraps and gingerbread, purses and pouches. There were booths and toyshops. Displayed 'at the sign

Kitchen Stuff

Young Radishes

Water Cresses

Live Whiting

Small Coal

Yorkshire Cakes

Shrimps

Knives to Gri

Spectacles

Work for the
Cooper

Rabbets O

Ripe Artichou

...read or Brass	Singing Birds	Evening Post	Milk Maids
...eet Oysters	Rope of Onions	Buy my Flounders	Hot Pies
...d Clouths	Sweep Soot O	Kentish Cherries	Buy any Pencils

of the Shoe and Slap' was 'THE WONDER OF NATURE, a girl about sixteen years of age, born in Cheshire, and not above eighteen inches long . . . Reads very well, whistles, and all very pleasant to hear.' Close by was exhibited 'a Man with one Head and two distinct Bodies', as well as a 'Giant Man' and 'Little Fairy Woman' performing among the other freak shows and theatrical booths. There were puppies, whistling birds and horses for sale; there were ballads cried out, with bottled ale and tobacco being constantly consumed. Cunning men cast nativities, and prostitutes plied their trade. Jonson himself noted small details, too, and watched as the cores of apples were gathered up for the bears. As one of his characters puts it, 'Bless me! deliver me, help, hold me! the Fair!'

It continued, curiously enough, during the Puritan Commonwealth, no doubt with the primary motive of venting the steam of the more unruly citizens, but flourished after the Restoration of 1660 when liberty and licence came back into fashion. One versifier of the period notes masquerades dramatising 'The Woman of Babylon, The Devil and The Pope', as well as shows of dancing bears and acrobats. Some acts came year after year: there was the 'Tall Dutchwoman' who made annual appearances for at least seventeen years, together with the 'Horse and no Horse, whose tail stands where his head should do'. And there were always rope-walkers, among them the famous Scaramouch 'dancing on the rope, with a wheelbar-row before him with two children and a dog in it, and with a duck on his head', and the notable rope-dancer Jacob Hall 'that can jump it, jump it'. Perhaps the most celebrated of all the acts, however, was that of Joseph Clark, 'the English Posture Master' or 'Posture Clark' as he was known. It seems that he could 'put out of joynt almost any Bone or Vertebra of his Body, and to re-place it again'; he could so contort himself that he became unrecognisable even to his closest friends. And so the fair went on, as all fairs do. There was even a Ferris wheel, known then as a 'Whirligig' (later an 'Up and Down') where, according to Ned Ward in *The London Spy* (1709), 'Children lock'd up in Flying Coaches who insensibly climb'd upwards . . . being once Elevated to a certain height come down again according to the Circular Motion of the Sphere they move in'.

The general noise and clamour, together with the inevitable crowd of pickpockets, finally proved too much for the city authorities. In 1708 the fortnight of the fair was reduced to three days at the end of August. But if it became less riotous, it was no less festive. Contemporary accounts dwell upon the drollery of 'merry Andrews', otherwise known as Jack Puddings or Pickled Herrings; they wore a costume with donkey's ears, and accompanied other performers with their fiddles. One of the more famous fools was a seller of gingerbread nuts in Covent Garden; since he was paid one guinea a day for his work at

Bartholomew Fair, held each August in the vicinity of Smithfield Market.

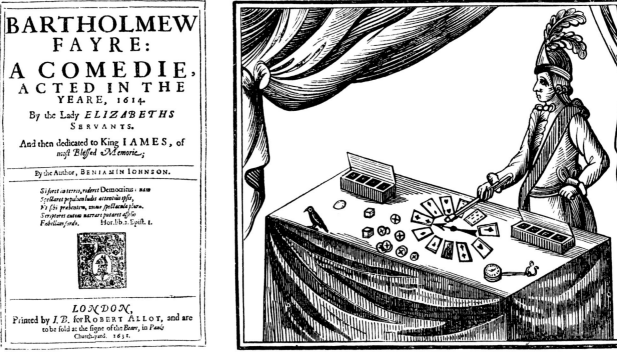

A nineteenth-century booth for Punch and Judy.

Bartholomew Fair, 'he was at pains never to cheapen himself by laughing, or by noticing a joke, during the other 362 days of the year'. And so the fair rolled on. It is perhaps appropriate, amid the noise and excitement, that in 1688 John Bunyan collapsed and died at the corner of Snow Hill and Cock Lane.

If there was one central character, however, it was that of Punch, the uncrowned monarch of 'puppet-plays, hobby-horses, tabors, crowds, and bag-pipes'. He had emerged upon the little stage by the end of the seventeenth century, announced by a jester and accompanied by fiddle, trumpet or drum. He is not a uniquely London phenomenon, but he became a permanent entertainer at the fairs and streets of the city; with his violence, his vulgarity and his sexual innuendo he was a recognisable urban character. 'Often turning towards a tightly packed bend of girls, he sits himself down near to them: My beautiful ones, he says, winking roguishly, here's a girl friend come to join you!' With his great belly, big nose and long stick he is the very essence of a gross sexual joke which, unfortunately, in later centuries became smaller, squeakier, and somehow transformed into entertainment for children. There is a watercolour by Rowlandson, dated 1785, which shows a puppet-play with Punch in action. George III and Queen Charlotte are driving to Deptford, but the attention of the citizens is drawn more towards the wooden booth where Punch is beating the bare buttocks of his wife. He was often conceived as a 'hen-pecked' husband but, here, the worm has turned. Rowlandson's work is of course partly conceived as a satire against the royal family, but it is filled with a greater and all-encompassing urban energy.

Within Bartholomew Fair itself there was a complete erasure of ordinary social distinctions. One of the complaints against it lay in the fact that apprentice and lord might be enjoying the same entertainments, or betting at the same gaming tables. This is entirely characteristic of London itself, heterogeneous and instinctively egalitarian. It is no coincidence, for example, that at the time of the Fair an annual supper was held in Smithfield for young chimney-sweeps. Charles Lamb has immortalised the occasion in one of his essays, 'The Praise of Chimney Sweepers', where he reports that 'hundreds of grinning teeth startled the night with their brightness' while in the background could be heard the 'agreeable hubbub' of the Fair itself. It might be argued that there is no true egalitarianism in the gesture, and that such solemn festivities merely accustom the little ''weeps' to their dismal fate. This might be considered one of the paradoxes of London, which consoles those it is about to consume.

London architects have understood the city's innate theatricality. Inigo Jones's construction

Miss A. Young, acrobat, known as the female Blondin, entertaining spectators on land and on water.

of the Banqueting House in 1622 was, in the words of John Summerson's Georgian London, 'really an extension of his stage work'; the same might be said of his other great urban projects. In a similar spirit, two hundred years later, John Nash disguised a concerted effort at town planning, dividing the poor of the east from the wealthy of the west, by creating streets and squares which represented the principles of 'picturesque beauty' by means of scenic effects. George Moore commented that the 'circular line' of Regent Street was very much like that of an amphitheatre, and it has been noted that the time of Nash's 'Improvements' was also the period of the great panoramas and dioramas of London. Buckingham Palace, as viewed from the end of the Mall, seems nothing more than an elaborate stage-set while the House of Commons is an exercise in wistful neo-Gothic not unlike the elaborate dramas to be seen in the patent theatres of the period. The latest Pevsner guide notes that much of the architecture of the 1960s 'took the expressive potential of concrete to a theatrical extreme'.

That central spirit of London has been divined by artists as well as architects. In the work of Hogarth the streets are delineated in terms of scenic perspective. In many of his prints, perhaps most notably in his delineation of the Fair, the division between performers and spectators is for all practical purposes invisible; the citizens fulfil their roles with even more animation than the stage actors, and there are more genuinely dramatic episodes among the crowd than upon the boards. Some of the more famous portraits of London also borrow their effects from the theatre of the period.

The rituals of crime have, in London, also taken on a theatrical guise. Jonathan Wild, the master criminal of mid-eighteenth-century London, declared that 'The mask is the summum bonum of our age' while the marshalmen, or city police of a slightly later date, were costumed in cocked hats and spangled buttons. There were more subtle disguises available to the detective of the city. One is reminded of Sherlock Holmes, a character who could have existed only in the heart of London. According to his amanuensis, Holmes 'had at least five small refuges in different parts of London, in which he was able to change his personality'.

If crime and detection rely upon disguise, so London punishment had its own theatre of judgement and of pain. The Old Bailey itself was designed as a dramatic spectacle, and was indeed compared with 'a giant Punch and Judy show' where the judges sat within the open portico of a Sessions House which resembled a theatrical backdrop. The cellar floor of the Fleet Prison was known as 'Bartholomew Fair', while in the chapel of Newgate there were galleries where spectators were invited to watch the antics of those condemned to die who deliberately entertained their audience with acts of outrageousness or defiance. We read, for example, of one John Riggleton who 'made a practice of sneaking up to the Ordinary [prison clergyman] when his eyes were fast shut in prayer and shouting out loud in his ear'. This of course is the role of the pantaloon in pantomime.

The theatre did not end in the prison chapel, but continued upon the little stage where the execution took place. 'The upturned faces of the eager spectators', wrote one contributor

'St Pancras Hotel and Station', in the 1880s, from the Pentonville Road. The artist, John O'Connor, was also an accomplished painter of theatrical scenery.

Painting inspired by Jonathan Swift's 'A Description of a City Shower'. The maid's mop is causing a problem.

Trial, execution and then further punishment by means of public dissection in the theatre of the Surgeons Hall at the Old Bailey. London has always been the city of spectacle.

to *The Chronicles of Newgate*, 'resembled those of the "gods" at Drury Lane on Boxing Night.' Another witness remarked upon the fact that, just before the execution, there was a roar of '"Hats off!" and "Down in front!" as at a theatre'. There was one peculiarly theatrical episode at the execution in 1820 of Thistlewood and his 'Cato Street' companions for treason; according to the traditional sentence, they were to be hanged and then beheaded. 'When the executioner had come to the last of the heads, he lifted it up, but, by some clumsiness, allowed it to drop. At this the crowd yelled out, "Ah, Butter-fingers!"' This small episode manifests the peculiar temperament of the London crowd, combining humour and savagery in equal measure.

The exploits of Jack Sheppard proved how intense could be the excitement aroused in London by the adventures of a criminal. The most notable painter of the day, Sir James Thornhill, visited him in 1724 in order to complete a portrait which was then sold to the public as a mezzotint. Nine years later, in 1732, Thornhill's son-in-law, William Hogarth, made a similar journey to Newgate; here he sketched another famous malefactor, Sarah Malcolm, herself held in the condemned cell. She had strangled two elderly parties, and then cut the throat of their maid, the recklessness of the crimes lending her notoriety among the London public. She was very young – only twenty-two – and very composed. At her trial she declared the blood on her shift to be the issue of menstruation rather than of murder and, after the sentence of death had been pronounced upon her, confessed that she was a Roman Catholic. Hogarth painted her sitting in her cell, her rosary beads before her, and announced in the public press that his print would be ready within two days. It was an advertisement of his skill as well as a tribute to the notoriety of his subject. Hogarth, it seems, could not resist the lineaments of the condemned. When in 1761 Theodore Gardelle was about to be hanged at the corner of Panton Street and the Haymarket, Hogarth captured his countenance of despair 'with a few swift strokes'.

It is of some interest, then, that in February 1728 Hogarth attended and enjoyed *The Beggar's Opera* by John Gay. In this drama the 'low' criminal life of London is presented in bright theatrical guise. A true London production, part burlesque and part burletta, it was a parody of fashionable Italian opera, as well as a satire upon governmental cabal. With its main characters of Macheath, a highwayman, and Peachum, a receiver of stolen goods, it aspired to be a spirited representation of the London criminal world appropriately completed by the portrait of Lockit, the keeper of Newgate. The dramatic scenes within Newgate itself confirm two of the city's most permanent images: the world as a stage and the world as a prison.

Sarah Malcolm, the murderess, portrayed by William Hogarth.

Scenes from 'The Beggar's Opera' by John Gay, a spoof opera in which London's low life and high life are compared.

Gay was accused of glamorising thieves and receivers of stolen goods, as if in the act of equalising the activities of the beggars and their 'betters' he was somehow lending vulgar distinction to the more disreputable elements of London life. It was reported by one contemporary moralist that 'several thieves and street robbers confessed in Newgate that they raised their courage at the playhouse by the songs of their hero Macheath, before they sallied forth in their desperate nocturnal exploits'. If that was indeed the case, then we see in the fervent and fevered context of London that street life feels no compunction in taking on the lineaments of dramatic art.

Hogarth saw the possibility of channelling his own genius through *The Beggar's Opera*. He painted the same scene from the play on six separate occasions, in the process, according to Jenny Uglow, 'bursting into life as a true painter'. It is not hard to understand how this intense depiction of London life invigorated and animated the artist, since in his subsequent work he reveals his own vital engagement with the scenic possibilities of street life. In fact he creates his own tradition of London villains, in the characterisation of 'Tom Nero' in *The Four Stages of Cruelty* (1751) and 'Thomas Idle' in the *Industry and Idleness* series (1747); both end as murderers, suspended on the gallows, but the course of their fatal careers is given a lurid and sensational aspect by being placed within the context of the streets and 'low' haunts of the city.

Everything there conspires to engender dreadful deeds, and, in *The Four Stages of Cruelty*, the life of the city itself is the true engine of that cruelty.

If John Gay was intent upon turning thieves or receivers into dramatic heroes or characters, then he was himself following a distinguished London tradition. In the four years before *The Beggar's Opera* had appeared on stage there had been other theatrical representations of *Harlequin Sheppard* and *A Match in Newgate*, the former suggesting a remarkable link between pantomime and crime. More than a century earlier Beaumont and Fletcher, in *The Beggar's Bush*, had given dramatic currency to the tricks and slang of London criminals.

The tradition continued in the sensational accounts of the lives of famous criminals, whose exploits were every bit as melodramatic as the characters upon the stage. There was the enormously popular *Newgate Calendar*, for instance, the general title given to a succession of books which began to emerge at the end of the eighteenth century. Its

et cantare pares et respondere parati

Harmon

Polly Peachum   Captain Macheath

popularity was such that it can be compared to Foxe's *Book of Martyrs* in the mid-sixteenth century or perhaps the ubiquitous legends about saints of the medieval period. It might even be compared to the vogue for fairy tales emerging in the early nineteenth century. The ambiguity of the genre is further compounded by the school of the 'Newgate novel' which emerged in the same period, with such celebrated practitioners as Harrison Ainsworth and Bulwer Lytton.

The content of these various publications was equally ambiguous, hovering somewhere between celebration and condemnation. In similar fashion skill and cunning, disguise and stratagem, were commonly admired as the dramatic expedients of street life. There was Mary Young, known as Jenny Diver, who practised in the London streets around 1700; she would dress up as a pregnant woman and, hiding a pair of artificial arms and hands beneath her dress, opened pockets and purses with ease. She, in turn, was celebrated by the London populace for her 'skills of timing, disguise, wit and dissimulation'.

But there were other, more callous criminals such as the nineteenth century master of disguise Charles Price, or 'Old Patch', who murdered anyone who got in their way. The celebration of their disguises is consequently tempered by disgust at the nature of their crimes. This indeed was a feature of *The Newgate Calendar* itself, as in 'A Narrative of the horrid Cruelties of Elizabeth Brownrigg on her Apprentices'. She was a midwife chosen by the overseers of the poor of St Dunstan's parish 'to take care of the poor women who were taken in labour in the workhouse'. She had several penniless girls working as her servants, at her house in Fleur-de-lis Court off Fleet Street, and she systematically tortured, abused and killed them. As she was led to her death, in the autumn of 1767, the London mob shouted out that 'she would go to hell' and that 'the devil would fetch her'. Her body was anatomised, and her skeleton displayed in a niche of Surgeon's Hall. There was also a great trade in 'Last Dying Confessions'. Some were genuinely composed by the felons themselves – who often took great delight in reading their 'Last Speeches' in their cells – but customarily it was the 'Ordinary' or religious minister of Newgate who wrote what were essentially morbid and moralistic texts. The city then became a stage upon which were presented spectacles for the delight and terror of the urban audience.

The connection of fact and fiction, in the realm of crime, was not wholly lost in the twentieth century. Tommy Steele played Jack Sheppard in *Where's Jack?*, Phil Collins was 'Buster' Edwards in *Buster*, Roger Daltrey was John McVicar in *McVicar* and two performers from Spandau Ballet enacted the Kray brothers in *The Krays*. The tradition of *The Beggar's Bush* and *The Beggar's Opera* continues.

London traders and shopkeepers. Many of them carried heavy burdens. From its foundation, London has been built upon commerce and upon trade.

Covent Garden
market, then and
now.

Previous page:
Women carrying
boxes of flowers,
1934. These three
were among the last
of the female
porters; they had
worked in the
flower market
respectively for
thirty-nine, forty-
two and forty years.
Men balancing
baskets.
Loading and
unloading goods,
circa 1900.

This page: Covent
Garden today by
Richard Foster.
With its re-designed
Opera House, wine
bars and street
performers, the
piazza is given over
to entertainment.

Images of prisoners in Wormwood Scrubs unusually showing both profile and full-front in one photograph taken in the 1880s. London itself has often been compared to a prison.

And of course there has always been something intensely theatrical about London crowds. The London crowd is not a single entity, manifesting itself on particular occasions, but the actual condition of London itself. The city is one vast throng of people. 'On looking into the street,' one seventeenth-century observer recalled, 'we saw a surging mass of people moving in search of some resting place which a fresh mass of sightseers grouped higgledy piggledy rendered impossible. It was a fine medley: there were old men in their dotage, insolent youths and boys . . . painted wenches and women of the lower classes carrying their children.' A 'medley' suggests a show or spectacle, and in the mid-seventeenth century painters began subtly to examine the London crowd.

There was always the speed, as well as the spectacle. We learn further from Pierre Jean Grosley's *A Tour to London* in 1772 that 'the English walk very fast; their thoughts being entirely engrossed by business, they are very punctual to their appointments, and those, who happen to be in their way, are sure to be sufferers by it; constantly darting forward, they justle them with a force proportioned to the bulk and velocity of their motion'.

And then, of course, there was the noise. There is something crude, and alarming, about the sound of the crowd; it is as if the voice of the city were primeval, unearthly. Yet sometimes its collective breath is charged with misery. On the day of the execution of Charles I, 30 January 1649, a great throng was assembled in Whitehall; at the instant of the blow which removed the king's head, 'there was such a Grone by the Thousands then present, as I never heard before & desire may never hear again'.

Yet, for the royalists of the seventeenth century, the throng of London were 'the scum of all the profanest rout, the vilest of all men, the outcast of the people . . . mechanic citizens, and apprentices'. The crowd, in other words, became a tangible threat; it was turning into a mob (the word was coined in the seventeenth century) which might become King Mob. The salient fact was that London had grown immeasurably larger in the sixteenth and seventeenth centuries, and so obviously the size of its crowds was enlarged. In 1668 there were riots in Poplar and in Moorfields, and the new prison at Clerkenwell was broken open by the people to rescue those who had been imprisoned for the old London custom of pulling down brothels. 'But here it was said,' noted Pepys, 'how these idle fellows have had the confidence to say that they did ill in contenting themselves in pulling down the little bawdy-houses and did not go and pull down the great bawdy house at Whitehall.' This is the authentic radical and levelling voice of the Londoner, newly become a crowd or throng or mob, in the heart of the city.

So London had become dangerous. 'When a mob of chairmen or servants, or a gang

'There was such a Grone by the thousands then present.' Eyewitness representation of the execution of King Charles 1.

Right: Crowds celebrating New Year's Eve, 1934. When does a crowd become a mob?

of thieves or sharpers, are almost too big for the civil authority,' wrote Henry Fielding, 'what must be the case in a seditious tumult or general riot?' The history of the eighteenth-century crowd displays a gradual change of temper which was disturbing to magistrates such as Fielding. The scorn and insults were no longer primarily levelled at strangers or outsiders but, rather, at those of wealth or authority. 'A man in court dress cannot walk the streets of London without being pelted with mud by the mob,' Casanova wrote in 1746, '. . . the Londoners hoot the king and the royal family when they appear in public.'

If you had any hope of finding 'a community life' in London, 'all foreigners' agree that it is as if you searched 'for flowers in a vale of sand'. There was no community in London in the eighteenth century, and no sense of communal life, only a number of distinctive and distinguishable crowds. There were crowds of women attacking bawdy houses or dishonest shops, crowds of citizens alerted by a 'hue and cry', crowds of parishioners attacking a local compter, crowds watching a fire, crowds of beggars, and, most ominously, crowds of distressed or unemployed workers. There were riots by silk-weavers and coal-heavers, hat-makers and glass-grinders, and a host of assorted tradesmen whom creeping industrialisation and increased food prices had rendered ever more desperate.

In the eighteenth century there are many accounts of mobs with lighted torches and sticks or clubs; their leaders would read out the names of people, or of specific streets, in order to direct the violence against local targets. Houses and factories and mills could be literally pulled down; looms were cut apart. Sometimes we can hear them shouting – 'Green you bugger, why don't you fire? We will have your heart and liver!' It is perhaps significant, in the context of the violent language of London, that much Cockney dialect springs immediately from pugilism: 'bread-basket' for stomach, 'kisser' for mouth, 'conk' for nose, 'pins' for legs and 'knock-aht' for a sensation.

The most violent and widespread riot in London history started as a demonstration against legislation in favour of Roman Catholics, but quickly turned into a general assault upon the institutions of the state and the city. On 2 June 1780, Lord George Gordon assembled four columns of his supporters in St George's Fields, in Lambeth, and led them to Parliament Square in order to protest against the Catholic Relief Act. The Annual Register of 1781, records that the day was intensely hot yet Gordon's supporters marched in the heat three abreast, the main column some four miles in length, and when they converged outside Westminster they raised a great yell. The heat now inflamed them, as they invaded the lobbies and passages of Parliament. Their petition was carried into the chamber of the House of Commons while, outside, the crowd screamed and yelled in triumph. But then a rumour spread that armed soldiers were advancing in readiness to confront them and they fled. As they did so a body of Horse Guards surrounded some of the rioters and escorted them as prisoners to Newgate; this removal was, as events demonstrated, an unfortunate one.

The mob dispersed, among a hundred rumours which resounded through the city, only to gather itself again as evening approached. Doors and windows were barred as the nervous citizenry prepared itself for further violence. The crowd had diverted its energies from Westminster to Lincoln's Inn Fields where a notorious 'mass house' was situated; it was in fact the private chapel of the Sardinian ambassador, but no diplomatic nicety could assuage the temper of the mob which burned it down and demolished its interior. So opened a path of destruction which would burn its way across London.

The next day, Saturday, was relatively quiet. On the following morning, however, a mob met in the fields near Welbeck Street and descended upon the Catholic families of Moorfields. There they burned out houses and looted a local Catholic chapel. On Monday the violence and looting continued, but now it was also directed against the magistrates involved in confining some of the anti-Catholic rioters to Newgate as well as against the politicians who had inaugurated the pro-Catholic legislation. It was not simply a 'No Popery' protest now but a concerted assault upon the established authorities.

According to Charles Dickens, who gave an account of the riots in Barnaby Rudge, 'The contagion spread like a dread fever: an infectious madness, as yet not near its height, seized on new victims every hour, and society began to tremble at their ravings.' The image of distemper runs through London's history; when it is combined with the imagery of the theatre, where each incendiary incident becomes a 'scene', we are able to glimpse the complicated life of the city.

There were now mobs all over the city; most citizens wore a blue cockade to signal

The authorities of
London were gener-
ally quick to dispel
disorder. It had a
habit of growing.

their allegiance to the rioters, and houses displayed a blue flag with the legend 'No Popery' inscribed upon their doors and walls. Most of the shops were closed, and throughout London there was fear of violence 'the like of which had never been beheld, even in its ancient and rebellious times'. Troops had been stationed at all the major vantage points, but they also seemed to be sympathetic to the cries and demands of the mob. The Lord Mayor felt unable, or was unwilling, to issue direct orders to arrest or shoot the rioters. So fires and destruction started up in various areas.

It was a vast army of the disadvantaged and the dispossessed turning upon the city with fire and vengeance. If ever London came close to a general conflagration, this was the occasion. After the houses of certain judges and law-makers had been burned down the crowd cried 'Now Newgate!'. The columns marched on the prison from all directions, from Clerkenwell and Long Acre, from Snow Hill and Holborn, and they assembled in front of its walls at a little before eight o'clock that Tuesday evening. They surrounded the house of the Keeper, Richard Akerman, which fronted the street beside the prison. A man appeared on the rooftop, asking what it was that they wanted. 'You have got some friends of ours in your custody, master.' 'I have a good many people in my custody.' One of the mob leaders, a black servant called John Glover, was heard to cry out: 'Damn you, Open the Gate or we will Burn you down and have Everybody out.' No satisfactory answer was given, and so the mob fell upon Akerman's house.

That great prison door was the focus of their early efforts; all the furniture of the Keeper's house was piled against it and, smeared with pitch and tar, was soon ablaze. It became a sheet of flame, burning so brightly that the clock of the church of the Holy Sepulchre could clearly be seen. Some scaled the walls and threw down blazing torches upon the roof. When the fire had taken hold of the prison the prisoners themselves were in peril of being burned alive. An eye-witness, Frederick Reynolds, recalled that 'The wild gestures of the mob without and the shrieks of the prisoners within, expecting instantaneous death from the flames, the thundering descent of huge pieces of building, the deafening clangour of red-hot iron bars striking in terrible concussion on the pavement below, and the loud, triumphant yells and shouts of the demoniac assailants on each new success, formed an awful and terrific scene'. Eventually the gate, charred and still in flames, began to give way; the crowd forced a path through the burning timbers and entered the gaol itself.

They ran down the stone passages, screaming exultantly, their cries mixing with the yells of the inmates seeking release and relief from the burning fragments of wood and the encroaching fire. Bolts and locks and bars were wrenched apart as if the strength of the mob

The Gordon Riots at their height. Illustrated by Phiz for Charles Dickens's 'Barnaby Rudge'.

had some unearthly vigour. Some were carried out exhausted and bleeding; some came out shuffling in chains and were immediately taken in triumph to a local blacksmith to the shrieks of 'A clear way! A clear way!' from the multitude who surrounded with joy those who had been released. More than three hundred prisoners were liberated. Some had escaped from imminent execution, and were like men resurrected; others were hurried away by friends; others, habituated to the prison, wandered in astonishment and bewilderment through the wreckage of Newgate. Other prisons were fired and opened that night, and it was – for that night, at least – as if the whole world of law and punishment had been utterly demolished. In subsequent years the Londoners of the area recalled the unearthly light which seemed to shine from the very stones and streets of the city. The city was momentarily transformed.

The following day became known as 'Black Wednesday'. It might almost have been termed Red Wednesday. That morning the 'cowardice' of London was manifest in the closed shops and shuttered windows. Many of the citizens were so dismayed and astounded by the destruction of Newgate, and the complete failure of the city authorities to punish or apprehend those who were responsible, that it seemed to them that the whole fabric of reality was being torn apart before their eyes. And 'round the smoking ruins people stood apart from one another and in silence, not venturing to condemn the rioters, or to be supposed to do so, even in whispers'. There was another curious aspect of this lawlessness. Some prisoners lately released sought out their gaolers, 'preferring imprisonment and punishment to the horrors of such another night as the last', while others actually returned to Newgate in order to wander among the smoking ruins of their erstwhile place of confinement. They were brought there by some 'indescribable attraction', according to Dickens, and they were found talking, eating and even sleeping in the places where their cells had once stood. It is a curious story but somehow all of a piece with the greater story of London, where many will dwell upon the same stones for the whole of their lives.

Troops had been stationed throughout the city, but the energy and purpose of the rioters were not significantly diminished. The leaders of the riot declared that they would take and fire the Bank, the Mint and the Royal Arsenal – and that they would occupy the royal palaces. A rumour spread that the demonstrators would also throw open the gates of Bedlam, thus contributing a curious terror to the general fear of the citizens. Truly then the city would become a hell with the desperate, the doomed and the distracted wandering its streets against buildings collapsing and houses on fire.

That night the rioters emerged upon the streets 'like a great sea', and it seemed their purpose 'to wrap the city in a circle of flame'. Thirty-six major fires were started – the prisons of the Fleet, the King's Bench and the Clink were all alight – while the soldiers fired upon the crowds with sometimes fatal effect. Some of the greatest conflagrations were in the vicinity of Newgate itself, beside Holborn Bridge and Holborn Hill, as if the destruction of the previous night had somehow magnetised the area so that it drew more vengeance upon itself. The spectacle of the burning city, again according to Johnson, created a 'universal panick'. There were sporadic riots on the next day, Thursday, but the incandescent scenes of the day before seem to have exhausted that lust for violence which had so suddenly visited the streets of London. The insurrection had passed as quickly and as generally as it had gathered just a week before. Two hundred were dead, more lying badly and often fatally injured, while no one was able to compute the numbers of those who had burned to death in cellars or hiding-places. Lord George Gordon was arrested and taken to the Tower of London, and hundreds of rioters were confined in the prisons that had not already been destroyed by fire. Twenty-five were hanged on the spots where their crimes had been committed; two or three boys were suspended before Lord Mansfield's house in Bloomsbury Square. So ended the most violent internecine episode in the city's history. Like all London violence it burned brightly but quickly, the stability and reality of the city being distorted by the heat of its flames before once more settling down.

There have been more prisons in London than in any other European city. From the penitential cell in the church of the Knights Templar to the debtors' prison in Whitecross Street, from the Clink situated in Deadman's Place, Bankside, to the compter in Giltspur Street, London has been celebrated for its places of confinement. There was a prison in Lambeth Palace where early religious reformers, the Lollards, were tortured, and a roundhouse in St Martin's Lane where twenty-eight 'were thrust into a hole six- feet square and kept there all night', four of the women being stifled to death. New prisons were always being built, from the Tun in Cornhill at the end of the thirteenth century to Wormwood Scrubs in East Acton at the end of the nineteenth. The prisoners were obliged to wear masks in the 'model prison' at Pentonville, while the 'new prison' of Millbank was supposed to have been built as a 'panopticon' whereby each cell and inmate could be individually scrutinised.

The Fleet was the oldest of them all, older even than Newgate, and had once been known as the 'Gaol of London'; it was also one of the first of the medieval city's stone buildings. The lowest 'sunken' storey was known as Bartholomew Fair, although the usual reports of brutality, immorality and mortality render it an ironic sobriquet. The prison was, however, most notorious for its 'secret' and unlawful marriages performed by 'degreaded clergymen' for less than a guinea. There was a watch-maker who impersonated a clergyman, calling himself 'Dr Gaynam' – or, perhaps, gain them. He resided in Brick Lane and it was his practice to walk up Fleet Street. Crossing Fleet Street Bridge 'in his silk gown and bands', he was known for his commanding figure, and a 'handsome though significantly rubicund face'. In the locality he was named as the 'Bishop of Hell'.

On several occasions the Fleet Prison was itself consigned to the flames, the last notable fire taking place in 1780 when a mob – led, perhaps appropriately, by a chimney-sweep - mounted an incendiary assult upon it. It was rebuilt in its old form, with many of its more interesting details left intact. Along what is now Farringdon Street, for example, the wall of the gaol had one open grating with bars across it. Here was placed an iron box for alms and, from within, one chosen inmate would call out perpetually 'Remember the poor prisoners'. This was the prison in which was incarcerated Samuel Pickwick who, after speaking to those who lay there 'forgotten' and 'unheeded', muttered: 'I have seen enough ... My head aches with these scenes, and my heart too.'

Scenes of prison life. There were more prisons in London than in any other city in the world.

The Fleet Prison was demolished in 1846, but the site was not cleared for another eighteen years. Where once were walls and cells there emerged 'blind alleys' which, even on summer days, were so narrow and crowded that they were 'bleak and shadowed'. The atmosphere of the ancient place lingered even after its material destruction.

It is likely that the Fleet inspired Thomas More's famous metaphor of the world as a prison, 'some bound to a poste ... some in the dungeon, some in the upper ward ... some wepying, some laughing, some labouring, some playing, some singing, some chiding, some fighting'.

More eventually himself became a prisoner, too, but, before that time, as under-sheriff of London, he had sent many hundreds of Londoners to gaol. He consigned some to the Old Compter in Bread Street and others to the Poultry Compter near Bucklersbury; in 1555 the prison in Bread Street was moved a few yards northward to Wood Street, where one of the inmates might have been echoing the words of Thomas More. He is quoted in Old and New London: 'This littel Hole is as a little citty in a commonwealth, for as in a citty there are all kinds of officers, trades and vocations, so there is this place as we may make a pretty resemblance between them.' The men consigned here were known as 'rats', the women as 'mice'. Its underground passages still exist beneath the ground of a small courtyard beside Wood Street; the stones are cold to the touch, and there is a dampness in the air. Once a new prisoner drank from 'a bowl full of claret' to toast his new 'society', and now the Compter is on occasion used for banquets and parties.

The image of the city as prison runs very deep. When Holloway Prison was opened in 1852 its entrance was flanked by two stone griffins which are, of course, also the emblems of the City of London. Its foundation stone carried the inscription 'May God preserve the City of London and make this place a terror to evil doers'.

Keir Hardie, on returning to his native Ayrshire in 1901, wrote that 'London is a place which I remember with a haunting horror, as if I had been confined there'. A report on London prisoners themselves, in London's Underworld by Thomas Holmes, in the very same period as Keir Hardie's observations, notes that 'the great mass of faces strikes us with dismay, and we feel at once that most of them are handicapped in life, and demand pity rather than vengeance'. The poverty in the city was such that 'the condition of prison life are better, as they need to be, than the conditions of their own homes'. So they simply moved from one prison to another. But gaol was the place, in Cockney idiom, 'where the dogs don't bite'.

The nineteenth century inherited all the propensities of the eighteenth century crowd but, in the enormous Oven or Wen, the crowd became increasingly impersonalised. Engels, the great observer of imperial London, remarked that 'the brutal indifference, the unfeeling isolation of each . . . is nowhere so shamelessly bare-faced . . . as just here in the crowding of the great city'. The nineteenth century crowd was also aware of itself as a new form of human congregation. W.P. Frith, endlessly depicted crowds in paintings which themselves attracted endless crowds. The London theatres were filled with melodramas in which the transient crowd was the characteristic setting for individual stories of pathos and violence. There is an account by George Gissing of the continuous movement 'of millions' on Jubilee Day (1887).

'Along the main thoroughfares of mid London where traffic was now suspended; between the houses moved a double current of humanity . . . a thud of footfalls numberless and the low unvarying sound that suggested some huge beast purring to itself in stupid contentment.' So the crowd becomes a beast, contented and obedient, wandering through the city which has created it.

Yet the city itself is curiously unmoved by its crowds. One of the reasons for civic peace in London, as opposed to other capitals, lies directly in its size. Its very scale determines its quietness. It is at once too large and too complex to react to any local outbreaks of passionate feeling, and in the twentieth century the most marked characteristic of riots and demonstrations was their failure to make any real impression upon the stony-hearted and unyielding city. The disappointment of the Chartist uprising in 1848, preceded by a large meeting on Kennington Common, anticipated the inability in 1936 of Oswald Mosley to proceed down Cable Street with thousands of fascist sympathisers. It was as if the city itself rebuked them and held them back. The poll tax riots of the late 1980s, around Whitehall and Trafalgar Square, were another instance of a violent local disturbance which did not affect the relative composure of the rest of the city. No movement could sweep through the entire capital, and no mob could ever control it. The city is so large, too, that it renders the average citizen powerless in its presence. In the early decades of the twentieth century there was something curiously compliant and complacent, not to say conservative, about the Cockneys; unlike the Parisians they did not want to fight the conditions of the city and were happy to live with them unchanged. That happy equilibrium could not last.

One unwelcome novelty of the latter half of the twentieth century, was the race riot, among the most notable being those of Notting Hill in 1958 and of Brixton in 1981. Another was the violence on council-house estates, of which the Broadwater Farm Estate disturbances of 1985 are perhaps the most terrible example. The disruption began in the autumn of 1985, upon a predominantly black council estate, where for several months there had been 'rumours of riots'. A series of separate incidents in the early autumn had exacerbated already emerging tensions. But the death of Mrs Cynthia Jarrett on the night of 5 October, allegedly while the police were searching her flat, precipitated the disturbances. The official report, Broadwater Farm Enquiry (1986), includes the statements of witnesses as well as descriptive analysis of the violence itself. 'So I thought: "Oh my God they down there and those children are there."' The actions of the police were reported in similar fashion. 'There was cries of "wait until we get in there and get you . . . get back in there, you bastards, get back in there"'. These could be the voices of any angry crowd, scattered across London over the past cen-

Riots have broken out throughout London's history, following approximately the same pattern and development. But the city is too large, and too impersonal, to be moved by them.

Previous page: Trafalgar Square; Victorian rioters. This page: 'Poll Tax riots', 1990.

turies, but it is incarnated here within a group of black youths confronted by lines of police in riot gear attempting to force them back upon the council estate as if they were prisoners being driven back into their cells.

'Some of the youths then began to turn over cars, and missiles were thrown at a line of police. Two cars were turned over and burned close to the junction. They attempted to turn over another car but were stopped . . . Soon after a wall at the corner of Willan Road and The Avenue was knocked down and dismantled for ammunition to throw at the police line. The fighting had started.' It spread rapidly, in characteristic fashion, and from the estate came 'constant volleys of dangerous missiles. Slabs of pavement were broken up and thrown. When the available slabs from nearby were used up, young people were seen rushing through the estate carrying missiles in various containers. A shopping trolley, a milk crate and a large communal rubbish bin were all mentioned to us as being used. At a later stage, tins stolen from the supermarket became a common form of ammunition.' Once more the common 'reality' of the city was being disrupted and changed. Crude and often ineffective petrol bombs were hurled at the encroaching police. 'Two people, both black, started shouting orders at the others: "we need more ammunition". Immediately five or six responded by running round the houses gathering up empty milk bottles, while four others turned over a car for petrol. In less than five minutes I counted more than 50 petrol bombs completed.'

One of the characteristics of accounts of the Gordon Riots was the allegation that secret managers exploited the violence and mayhem for their own ends. On Broadwater Farm the same phenomenon emerged. 'They were outsiders doing it to our Estate,' a witness explained, suggesting in turn that there are some people who relish urban conflagration for its own sake or as a means of affecting the entire social and political system. The fact that these strange organisers were apparently white, as witnessed by others, may suggest that sixth columnists wanted to inflame hatred against the black Londoners who lived upon the estate.

Yet the general movement of the crowd was as ever one of controlled confusion. The historian of rioting noted that 'Most of the people were united by a sense of anger which regularly escalated to fury. In this situation a dramatic cast, representative of any cross-section of society, was clearly evident.' Here his understanding of the patterns of riot comes into play, with his reference to 'a dramatic cast' as if it were part of London's theatre. He noticed some who tried to establish a plan of concerted action and impose order upon incipient chaos. But they were not wholly successful. 'In this sense,' he concluded, 'organisation was extemporised.' These are precisely the sentiments expressed by those who watched the unfolding of the Gordon Riots, and they suggest a great truth about violence in the city.

After the first confrontation there was no sustained attack but intermittent forays. Cars were overturned and shops looted. 'I discovered he was an Irish boy and he said that it's the first time he has had so much food in six months because he's unemployed.' Yet the most violent incident took place in the Tangmere precinct of the estate. One of the policemen despatched to guard the fire-fighters putting out a blaze in a newsagent's shop, PC Keith Blakelock, slipped and fell in the face of a pursuing mob. D. Rose, in *A Climate of Fear*, takes up the narrative. 'The rioters came at Blakelock from all sides . . . he was kicked on the ground and stabbed again and again.' Here we have an example of the sudden viciousness of a London mob. An observer described them as 'a pack of dogs . . . the instruments were going up and down being flayed at him. The last I saw of PC Blakelock was he had his hand up to protect himself . . . Blakelock's hands and arms were cut to ribbons . . . His head seems to have turned to one side, exposing his neck. There he took a savage cut from a machete.' And there he died.

It was another terrible episode in the history of London violence, where all the rituals of blood and vengeance have their place. The Tangmere precinct itself 'is a big, squat building, shaped in conscious imitation of a Babylonian ziggurat'. Babylon is ever associated with paganism and savagery. There were gunshots, and sporadic fires started upon the estate, but by midnight the rioters had begun to disperse. It started to rain. The violence ended as quickly and as suddenly as it had begun except, that is, for examples of brutality among the police towards various unnamed and still unknown suspects. That same pattern of vengeance was no doubt also part of the aftermath of the Gordon Riots.

It would be absurd to declare that these two events, separated by two hundred years, are identical in character and in motive. The fact that one was on a general and the other on a local scale, for example, is a comment on London's huge expansion over that period. One travelled along the streets, and the other was confined to the precincts of a council estate; this also testifies to changes within the society of London. Yet both sets of riots were against the power of the law, symbolised by the walls of Newgate Prison in the one case and by the ranks of police officers in riot gear in the other. It might be said that both therefore reflect a deep unease about the nature and presence of authority. The Gordon rioters were generally poor, part of the forgotten citizenry of London, and the inhabitants of the Broadwater Farm Estate were, according to Stephen Inwood, predominantly 'homeless, unemployed or desperate'. There may, again, be a connection. In both cases, however, the riots burned themselves out fierily and quickly. They had no real leaders. They had no real purpose except that of destruction. Such is the sudden fury of London.

In the Spring of 1981 the young black Londoners of Brixton, enraged by the perceived prejudice and oppression of the local police, erupted in street rioting. For the first time petrol bombs were used in attacks upon the police, together with the conventional deployment of bottles and bricks.

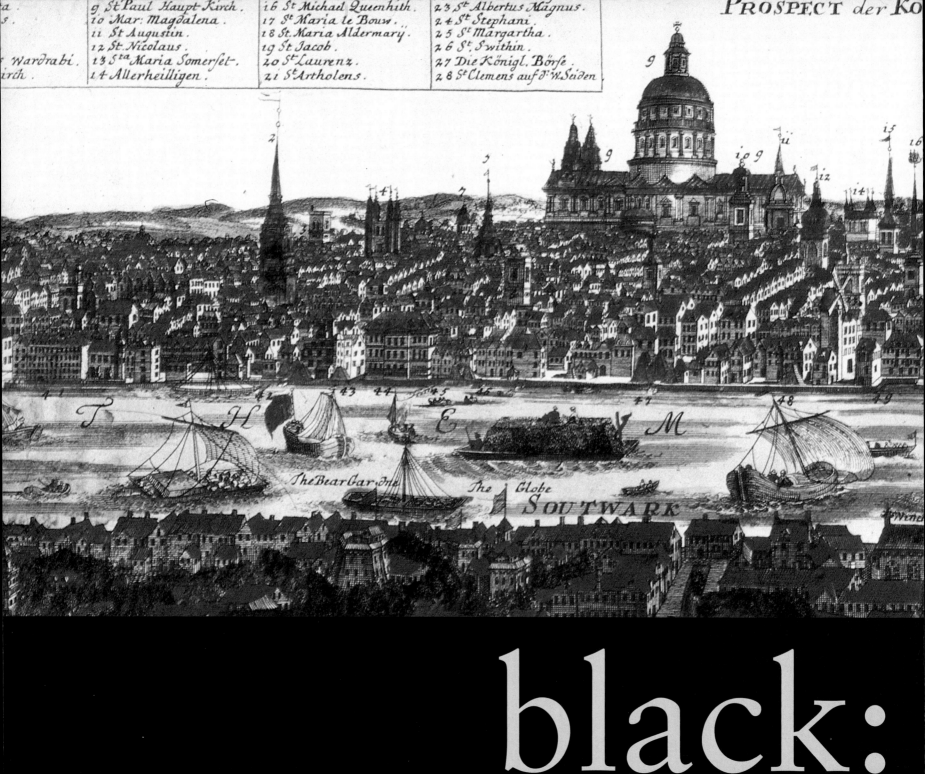

PROSPECT der Ko

The Bear Gar dne   The Globe SOUTWARK

black:

ondon became the city of empire – visible
xpression of unrivalled strength and immensity.

The eighteenth-century city stretched out to the west and to the east. By 1715 the scheme of building Cavendish Square, as well as certain streets to the north of the Tyburn Road, was first suggested. Then came Henrietta Street and Wigmore Road, the development of which prompted the extraordinary growth of Marylebone. In the 1730s Berkeley Square emerged on the western side. Bethnal Green and Shadwell were built up in the east, Paddington and St Pancras to the west.

A view of Devonshire Square, first laid out in the late seventeenth century.

DEVONSHIRE SQUARE

The maps grew denser, too, so that one square of the 1799 map covered six squares of the 1676 map. 'I have twice been going to stop my coach in Piccadilly, thinking there was a mob', wrote Horace Walpole in 1791, only to realise that it was the usual Londoners 'sauntering or trudging' down the thoroughfare. 'There will soon be one street from London to Brentford,' he complained, 'and from London to every village ten miles round.' He was announcing a law of life itself. The direct consequence of power and wealth is expansion. The eighteenth-century 'improvements' within the capital were also an aspect of that power and wealth. Lincoln's Inn Fields was enclosed in 1735 and, four years later, the increasingly squalid Stocks Market was removed from the centre of the city.

And then there was Westminster Bridge, opened in the winter of 1750 to the accompaniment of trumpets and kettledrums. Its fifteen arches of stone spanned the river to create 'a bridge of magnificence'. It had a decisive effect upon the appearance of the city in another sense, since its commissioners persuaded Giovanni Canaletto to visit London in order to paint it. It was still in the course of construction when he depicted it in 1746, but already his vision of London was tempered by his Venetian practice. London became subtly stylised, Italianate, stretching out along the Thames in a pure and even light. A city aspiring to fluency and grace had found its perfect delineator.

Canaletto's paintings show an idealised city aspiring towards magnificence.

Left: 'The Thames from the Terrace of Somerset House'.

Right: Lambeth Palace, the London home of the Archbishops of Canterbury since the end of the twelfth century.

From the middle of the eighteenth century London expanded in a fitful and almost feverish manner according to a cycle of profit and profiteering. The metaphor of fever was taken up by Henry Kett who, in 1787, suggested that 'The contagion of the building influenza . . . has extended its virulence to the country where it rages with unabating violence . . . The chain of buildings so closely unites the country with the town that the distinction is lost between Cheapside and St George's Fields. This idea struck the mind of a child, who lived at Clapham, with so much force, that he observed, "If they go on building at such a rate,

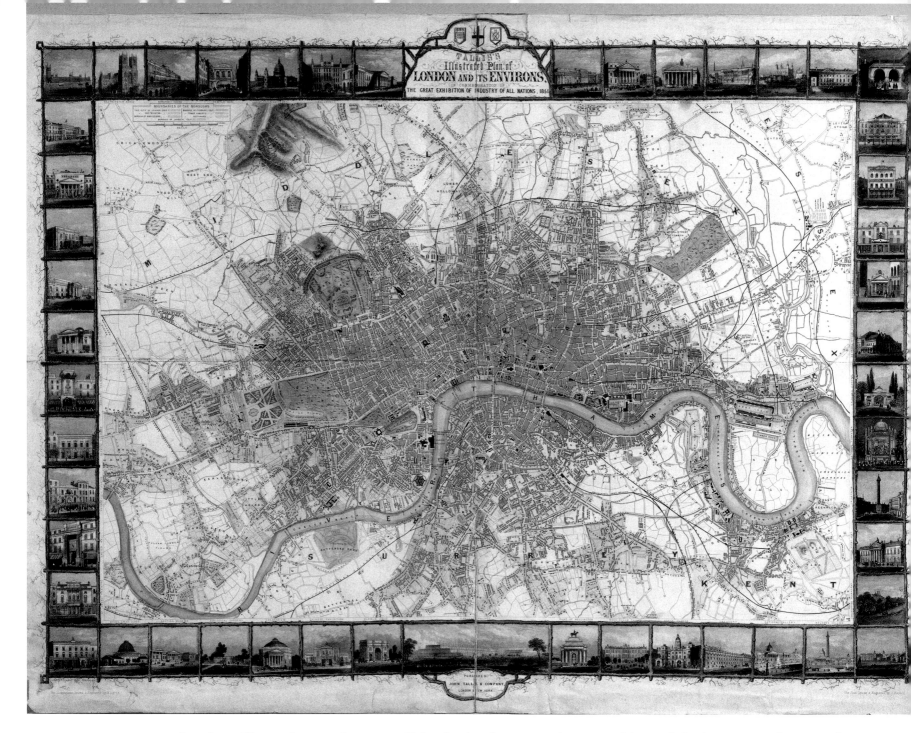

The map of London in 1851; the city was already spiralling out of control.

London will soon be next door to us."' By the time he grew to be a man, his words had come to pass.

The 'hills of Hampstead' were in part threatened by the 'New Road' from Paddington to Islington, upon which work began in 1756; it acted as a bypass, avoiding the congeries of narrow and unpaved roads which led to the centre of the city, and for a while was considered to be a northern perimeter road, acting as a barrier between the city and the country. But then the city, almost in a bound, travelled to its other side with the erection of Somers Town and Pentonville, Camden Town and Kentish Town. The new road became a road within, rather than outside, the city; and as such it remains.

The 'marshes of Lambeth' were invaded by a more deliberate act of policy, designed to increase the speed of business within the city and to open up the capital to its outer regions. Until 1750 only London Bridge acted as a conduit between the northern and southern areas of the Thames; the river itself was at the centre of all traffic. But the construction of Westminster Bridge over a period of twelve years entirely changed the relationship between the northern and southern sections; instead of being isolated and apart, almost like different countries sharing the same border, they became interrelated. A new road was built from the bridge into Lambeth for some half a mile, where it then touched existing roads which were in turn extended and widened in order to create a free-flowing route 'for promoting the intercourse and commerce' between both parts of the city. In the process both Kent and Surrey became so accessible that much open country disappeared beneath streets and squares.

The experiment was so profitable that four other bridges followed at Blackfriars, Vauxhall, Waterloo and Southwark. London Bridge itself was stripped of its houses and shops in order to render it suitable for the faster movement of a new age. Everyone was going faster. Everything was going faster. The city was growing faster, too, and the traffic within its bounds was moving ever more rapidly, starting a momentum which has never stopped. By the latter half of the eighteenth century the evidence of London's commercial power, and future imperial status, was already present. It was about to burst its bounds completely, and become the first metropolis of the world. So almost by instinct the old boundaries and gateways were destroyed; in a symbolic act of relinquishment, London prepared for its future.

The population itself expanded to meet London's demands, so that a figure of 650,000 in 1750 had reached over a million fifty years later. It was not until 1790 that baptisms exceeded burials, but from that time forward the momentum could not be stopped. In each of the five succeeding decades, after 1800, the population would rise by 20 per cent.

By the mid-1840s London had become known as the greatest city on the earth, the capital of empire, the centre of international trade and finance, a vast world market into which the world poured. Charles Dickens, Henry Mayhew and Friedrich Engels are three of the Victorian city-dwellers who cried 'havoc' over the exhaustive and exhausting city. In contemporary photographs and drawings the most striking images are those of labour and suffering. Women sit with their arms folded, hunched over; a beggar family sleep upon stone benches in a recess of a bridge, with the dark shape of St Paul's looming behind them. As Blanchard Jerrold put it, 'The aged, the orphan, the halt, the blind, of London would fill an

MICROCOSM dedicated to the London Water Companies.

MONSTER SOUP commonly called THAMES WATER, being a correct representation of that precious stuff doled out to us!!!

THE "SILENT HIGHWAY"-MAN.

"Your MONEY or your LIFE!"

ordinary city.' This is a strange conception, a city entirely composed of the maimed and injured. But that is, in part, what London was. The number of children and tramps, too, sitting resignedly in the street, is infinite; infinite also are the street-sellers, generally depicted against a dull background of brick or stone.

Yet there is another aspect of the Victorian city that photographs and images evoke: of vast throngs innumerable, the streets filled with teeming and struggling life, the great inspiration for the work of nineteenth-century mythographers such as Marx and Darwin. There are also flashes of feeling – of pity, anger, and tenderness – to be observed upon passing faces. And all around them can be imagined a hard unyielding noise, like an unending shout. This is Victorian London.

'Victorian London' is of course a general term for a sequence of shifting patterns of urban life. In the early decades of the nineteenth century, for example, it still retained many of the characteristics of the last years of the previous century. It was still a compact city. 'Draw but a little circle above the clustering housetops,' the narrator of Dickens's Master Humphrey's Clock suggests (1840-1), 'and you shall have within its space everything, with its opposite extreme and contradiction close by.' It was still only partially illuminated by gas and most of the streets were lit by infrequent oil-lamps with link-boys bearing lights to escort late pedestrians home. It was still hazardous. The outskirts retained a rural aspect; there were strawberry fields at Hammersmith and at Hackney, and the wagons still plied their way among the other horse-drawn traffic to the Haymarket. The great public buildings, with which the seat of empire was soon to be decorated, had not yet arisen. The characteristic entertainments were those of the late eighteenth century, too, with the dogfights, the cockfights, the pillory and the public executions. The streets and houses all contained plastered and painted windows, as if they were part of a pantomime. There were still strolling pedlars hawking penny dreadfuls, and ballad-singers with the latest 'air'; there were cheap theatres and print-shops displaying in their windows caricatures which could always catch a crowd. It was a more eccentric city. The inhabitants had had no settled education and no social 'system' (a word which itself did not spring into full life until the 1850s and 1860s) had yet been introduced. So it was a more varied, more unusual, and sometimes more alarming city than any of its successors. It had not yet been standardised, or come under the twin mid-Victorian agencies of uniformity and propriety.

It is impossible to gauge when this transformation occurred. Certainly London took on quite another aspect when it continued to grow and stretch itself through Islington and St John's Wood in the north; then through Paddington, Bayswater, South Kensington, Lambeth,

Opposite: 'The Bitter Tears of Outcast London'.

Following pages: These photographs, from the book entitled 'Street Life in London' by Adolph Smith, published in 1877, were taken by John Thompson 'to bring before the public some account of the present condition of the London street folk'. They are among the earliest examples of photography as social documentary.

The workers and trades of nineteenth-century London. The city was built upon the labour of its poor.

The building of the Metropolitan Line, 1867, the first underground railway system in the world.

Clerkenwell, Peckham and all points of the compass. It became the largest city in the world, just at the time when England itself became the first urbanised society in the world. It became the city of clock-time, and of speed for its own sake. It became the home of engines and steam-driven industry; it became the city where electromagnetic forces were discovered and publicised. It also became the centre of mass production, with the impersonal forces of demand and supply, profit and loss, intervening between vendor and customer. In the same period business and government were supervised by a vast army of clerks and book-keepers who customarily wore uniform dark costumes.

The construction of the Rotherhithe Tunnel, 1906. London has more passages beneath its river than any other capital city.

The railway tracks leading to King's Cross Station, opened in 1851 as part of the Great Northern Railway.

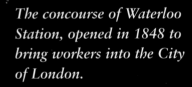

*The concourse of Waterloo
Station, opened in 1848 to
bring workers into the City
of London.*

*The roof of
St Pancras Station
under construction
in the 1860s.*

It was the city of fog and darkness but in another sense, too, it was packed to blackness. A population of one million at the beginning of the century increased to approximately five million by its close. By 1911, it had risen to seven million. Everything was becoming darker. The costumes of the male Londoner, like those of the clerks, switched from variegated and bright colours to the solemn black of the frock-coat and the stove-pipe hat. Gone, too, was the particular gracefulness and colour of the early nineteenth-century city; the decorous symmetry of its Georgian architecture was replaced by the imperialist neo-Gothic or neo-classical shape of Victorian public buildings. They embodied the mastery of time as well as that of space. In this context, too, there emerged a London which was more massive, more closely controlled and more carefully organised. The metropolis was much larger, but it had also become much more anonymous; it was a more public and splendid city, but it was also a less human one.

Thus it became the climax, or the epitome, of all previous imperialist cities. It became Babylon. There was in the twelfth century a part of London Wall called 'Babeylone', but the reasons for that name are unclear; it may be that in the medieval city the inhabitants recognised a pagan or mystical significance within that part of the stone fabric. Yet the

Battersea Power station at night, designed by Sir Giles Scott and opened in 1937. The towers rise three hundred feet into the air.

association or resemblance became pressing only in the nineteenth century when London was continually described as 'modern Babylon'. Henry James referred to it as 'this murky Babylon' and, for Arthur Machen, 'London loomed up before me, wonderful, mystical as Assyrian Babylon, as full of unheard-of things and great unveilings'. So Babylon has many associations; it conjures up images of magnitude and darkness, but also intimations of mystery and revelation. In this great conflation, even the gardens of Park Lane became known as the 'hanging gardens', although some echo may be found here of the Tyburn tree which was once located beside them.

By 1870 the sheer quantity of life in the city was overwhelming. Every eight minutes, of every day of every year, someone died in London; every five minutes, someone was born. There were forty thousand costermongers and 100,000 'winter tramps'; there were more Irish living in London than in Dublin, and more Catholics than in Rome. There were 20,000 public houses visited by 500,000 customers. Eight years later there were more than half a million dwellings, 'more than sufficient to form one continuous row of buildings round the island of Great Britain'. It is perhaps not surprising that mid-nineteenth-century Londoners were themselves struck with awe, admiration or anxiety at the city which seemed without any apparent warning to have grown to such magnitude and complexity. How could it have happened? Nobody seemed quite sure. Frederick Engels, in his *The Condition of the Working Classes in England in 1844* (1845), found his own considerable intellectual faculties to be strained beyond use. 'A town such as London,' he wrote, 'where a man may wander for hours together without reaching the beginning of the end . . . is a strange thing.' The strange city is indescribable, and so Engels could only resort to continual images of immensity. He writes of 'countless ships', 'endless lines of vehicles', 'hundreds of steamers'. The sheer incalculability of the mass seems to render it also unintelligible, and therefore induces fear.

So great was London that it seemed to contain within itself all previous civilisations. Babylon was then joined with other empires. The naves and transepts of Westminster Abbey were compared to the City of the Dead beyond Cairo, while the railway terminus at Paddington invoked images of the pyramid of Cheops. And beyond Egypt there was Rome. The subterranean vaults beneath the Adelphi reminded one architectural historian of 'old Roman works' while the sewer system of Joseph Bazalgette was often compared with the Roman aqueducts.

But there were other associations. Verlaine suggested that it was 'a Biblical city' ready for the 'fire of heaven' to strike it. Carlyle described it in 1824 as an 'enormous Babel . . . and the flood of human effort rolls out of it and into it with a violence that almost appals

The portico of Euston Station, built in 1838. London had become the new Rome.

It was demolished in 1961. London is always being destroyed and rebuilt.

one's very sense'. So in one context it is compared with the greatest civilisations of the past, with Rome or Egypt, and yet in another it is quickly broken down into a violent wilderness, a savage place, without pity or restraint of any kind. When Carlyle adds that London is also 'like the heart of all the universe', there is a suggestion that London is an emblem of all that is darkest, and most extreme, within existence itself. Is it the heart of empire, or the heart of darkness? Or is one so inseparable from the other that human effort and labour become no more than the expression of rage and the appetite for power?

In the nineteenth century the connotations of wilderness changed from unconstrained and uncurtailed life to one of barren desolation. The city is what Mayhew called 'a bricken wilderness', and the image of dense cover is replaced by one of hard stone with 'its profuse rank undergrowth of low, mean houses spreading in all directions'. This is the nineteenth-century desert, far larger and far more desolate than that of the eighteenth century.

There is one more salient aspect to this continual analogy of London with ancient civilisations: it is the fear, or hope, or expectation that this great imperial capital will in its turn fall into ruin. That is precisely the reason for London's association with pre-Christian cities; it, too, will revert to chaos and old night so that the condition of the 'primeval' past will also be that of the remote future. It represents the longing for oblivion. In Doré's vivid depiction of nineteenth-century London – London, essentially, as Rome or Babylon – there is an endpiece. It shows a cloaked and meditative figure sitting upon a rock beside the Thames. He looks out upon a city in awful ruin, the wharves derelict, the dome of St Paul's gone, the great offices simply piles of jagged stone. It is entitled 'the New Zealander' and derives its inspiration from Macaulay's vision of a 'colonial' returning to the imperial city after its destiny and destruction were complete; he wrote of the distant traveller as one 'who shall take his stand on the broken arch of London Bridge to sketch the ruins of St Paul's'. It is a vision which, paradoxically, emerged during the period of London's pride and greatness.

In many works of nineteenth-century fiction, characters stand upon an eminence, such as Primrose Hill or Fish Street Hill, and are struck into silence by the vision of the city's immensity. Macaulay acquired the reputation of having walked through every street in London but by the year of his death, in 1859, it was unlikely that anyone would have been able to reproduce that feat of pedestrianism. Here was a source of anxiety for an indigenous Londoner. He or she would never know all of the city thoroughly; there would always be a secret London in the very act of its growth. It can be mapped, but it can never be fully imagined. It must be taken on faith, not on reason.

There was a disconcerting sensation, much remarked upon, that a strange city was emerging ineluctably like a phantom in a mist. And it was changing everything that it touched. The concerted impulse to create a gigantic London – to widen streets, to put up great monuments, to create museums and law courts meant a chaos of demolition and reconstruction, with entire areas becoming building sites complete with hoardings and heavy machinery. The Holborn Viaduct was built to span the valley of the Fleet, linking Holborn Circus with Newgate Street; the great enterprise of the Victoria Embankment transformed the northern bank of the river and was extended into the heart of the city by Queen Victoria. Victoria Street transformed all of Westminster, while Shaftesbury Avenue and Charing Cross Road created the 'West End' as it is commonly understood. The City itself was steadily being depopulated, as bankers and merchants moved out to Kensington or Belgravia, until it became nothing but a counting-house. 'This monster London is really a new city,' Charles Eliot Pascoe wrote in 1888, 'new as to its life, its streets and the social conditions of the millions who dwell in them, whose very manners, habits, occupations and even amusements have undergone as complete change within the past half-century as the great city itself.' This is one aspect of London which the nineteenth century thoroughly revealed; the city itself changes its inhabitants, for better or worse, and actively intervenes in their lives. From that, of course, may spring a sense of oppression or imprisonment.

Yet there was a genuine feeling of awe concerning the vast extent of the city, as if a quite new thing had been created in the world. Where some saw only poverty and deprivation, others saw intelligence and industry; where some recognised only shabbiness and ugliness, others noted the blessings of trade and commerce. In effect London was now so large that practically any opinion could be held of it, and still be true. It was the harbinger

Steeplejacks during the creation of the Shell-Mex Building by the Thames. Originally a hotel, it was remodelled in 1930.

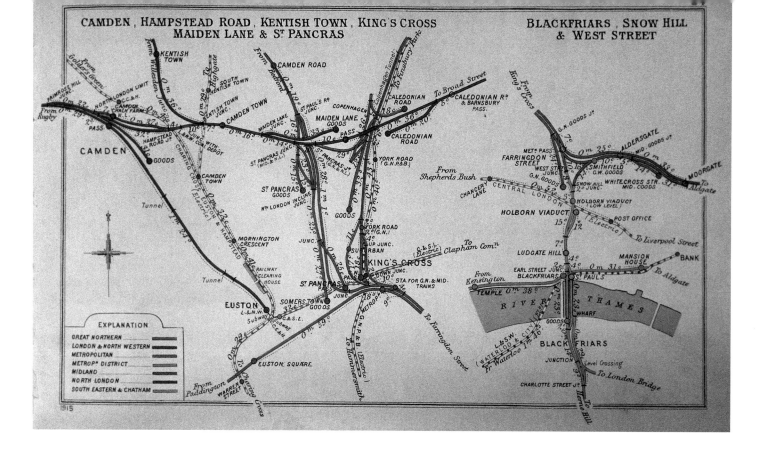

of a consumer society. It represented energy, and zeal, and inventiveness. But it was also the 'Great Wen', a monstrous growth filled with 'the bitter tears of outcast London'.

Another aspect of its size, therefore, was the fact that it contained everything. When Henry Mayhew ascended above London in a balloon he observed 'that vast bricken mass of churches and hospitals, banks and prisons, palaces and workhouses, docks and refuges for the destitute' all 'blent into one immense black spot . . . a mere rubbish heap' containing 'vice and avarice and low cunning' as well as 'noble aspirations and human heroism'. But in such a vast metropolis, forever growing, 'vice' and 'heroism' become themselves unimportant; the sheer size of London creates indifference.

This, in a sensitive mind such as that of Henry James, can lead to acute depression or feelings of estrangement. 'Up to this time,' he wrote to his sister in 1869, 'I have been crushed under a sense of the sheer magnitude of London – its inconceivable immensity – in such a way as to paralyse my mind . . . The place sits on you, broods on you, stamps on you.' That is another aspect of its unimaginable size; it acts as a giant weight or burden upon each individual life and consciousness. It is not simply that the citizens were literally dwarfed by the huge blocks and intricate machinery of the Victorian city, but rather that the sheer scale of London haunted its inhabitants. No one could ever memorise a map of Victorian London with its streets packed so tightly together that they could hardly be made out; it was beyond human capacity. But a place of such vastness, without limit, is also horrifying. It weighs upon the mind. It may lead to desperation, or release energy.

One of the characteristics of London faces was the appearance of tiredness. To journey through the city was itself fatiguing enough; it had grown too large to be manageable.

Above: Trains and 'the tube' carried workers into the city.

Right: Dock-workers at the end of their shift, 1939. The London docks were then the greatest employer of London labour.

London transport.
The city has always been
overcrowded with
passengers and traffic.

The crowds of Oxford
Street and London Bridge.
Different epochs, but the
phenomenon remains the
same. The crowd is
London's true family.

Below left: The trek to
work along the London
embankment, during the
General Strike.

The Londoner returned home exhausted, spiritless, dead to the world. So London wears out its citizens; it drains them of their energies, like a succubus. Yet for some 'this senseless bigness', as Henry James described it, was a source of fascination. Disraeli's vision of a vast uniformity was reversed in that context, because the absence of limits could also mean that everything is there; there were myriad shapes to be discerned, an endless profusion and prodigality of scenes and characters.

'When I came to this great city,' an African traveller wrote, 'I looked this way and that way; there is no beginning and no end.' He could have walked through Kennington and Camberwell, Hackney and Bethnal Green, Stoke Newington and Highbury, Chelsea and Knightsbridge and Kensington without ceasing to marvel. Between 1760 and 1835 the development rivalled that of the preceding two hundred years. By the latter date streets and terraces had reached Victoria, Edgware, the City Road, Limehouse, Rotherhithe and Lambeth. In the next sixteen years alone the city conquered Belgravia, Hoxton, Poplar, Deptford, Walworth, Bethnal Green, Bow Road and St Pancras. By 1872 it had expanded exponentially again to encompass Waltham Green, Kensal Green, Hammersmith, Highgate, Finsbury Park, Clapton, Hackney, New Cross, Old Ford, Blackheath, Peckham, Norwood, Streatham and Tooting, all of it growing and coming together beyond any civic or administrative control. London colonised each village or town as it encompassed them, making them a part of itself, but not necessarily changing their fundamental topography. They were now London, but they retained streets and buildings of an earlier date. Their old structure can just be recognised in the remains of churches, marketplaces and village greens, while their names survive as the titles of Underground stations.

It was often said that all England had become London, but some considered London to be an altogether separate nation with its own language and customs. For others London corresponded to the great globe itself or 'the epitome of the round world', as one nineteenth-century novelist put it. It is an indication of its prodigiousness, when such a great mass exerts its own form of gravity and attraction – 'lines of force', Thomas De Quincey called them in an essay entitled 'The Nation of London'.

Ordinary human existence seems uninteresting or unimportant in this place where everything is colossal. 'No man ever was left to himself for the first time in the streets, as yet unknown, of London,' De Quincey continued, 'but he must have been saddened and mortified, perhaps terrified, by the sense of desertion and utter loneliness which belongs to his situation.' Nobody regarded De Quincey; nobody saw or heard him. The people rushing past, bent upon their own secret destinations and contemplating their own hurried business,

'Before the Hurricane, Regent Street' by Bill Jacklin. London creates its own weather. The 'circular line' of Regent Street, reminiscent of an amphitheatre.

Were there no poor, then there would be no rich. Like the women who accompanied eighteenth-century armies, dependent and defenceless, so do the poor accompany London on its progress. It created the poor; it needed the poor, not least for the purpose of cheap or casual labour; now they have become the shadows which follow it everywhere.

The most visible manifestations of poverty came to London in the form of mendicants and beggars. They were arguing with each other at the end of the fourteenth century. 'John Dray in his own person denied the charge, and said that on the day and in the place mentioned he and the said Ralph were sitting together and begging, when John Stowe, a monk of Westminster came by and gave them a penny in common. Ralph received the penny, but would not give Dray his share. A quarrel arose and Ralph assaulted him with a stick.' Such a scene could have occurred centuries before, or centuries after. Where else could a beggar find a better plot than London itself, filled with people and according to legend replete with money?

There were religious mendicants, or hermits, mumbling in stone alcoves beside the principal gates of the city; there were lame beggars on street corners; there were prison beggars, calling out for alms from the gratings which held them; there were old women begging outside churches; there were children begging in the street. In the early twenty-first century some of the principal thoroughfares are lined with beggars, young and old; some lie huddled in doorways, wrapped in blankets, and stare up with imploring faces with the customary cry, 'Spare any change?' The older of them tend to be drunken vagrants, existing altogether out of time; which is as much to say that they uncannily resemble their counterparts in previous ages of London's history.

Charles Lamb wrote an essay in the 1820s, entitled 'A Complaint of the Decay of Beggars in the Metropolis', which remarked upon one of those sporadic and inconclusive attempts by the civic authorities to 'clear the streets'; there have through the centuries been proclamations and policies, but the beggars always return. Lamb in elegiac mood, however, anticipated their passing. 'The mendicants of this great city were so many of her sights, her lions. I can no more spare them than I could the cries of London. No corner of the street is complete without them. They are as indispensable as the ballad-singer, and in their picturesque attire as ornamental as the signs of old London.' The beggar somehow embodies the city, perhaps because he or she is an eternal type; like the games and songs of children, endlessly recurrent. As Lamb suggests, the beggar 'is the only man in the universe who is not obliged to study appearances. The ups and downs of the world concern him no longer.' Beyond the fleeting appearances of the world he represents unchanging identity.

The area of Whitechapel, from Charles Booth's 'Poverty Map' of 1902.

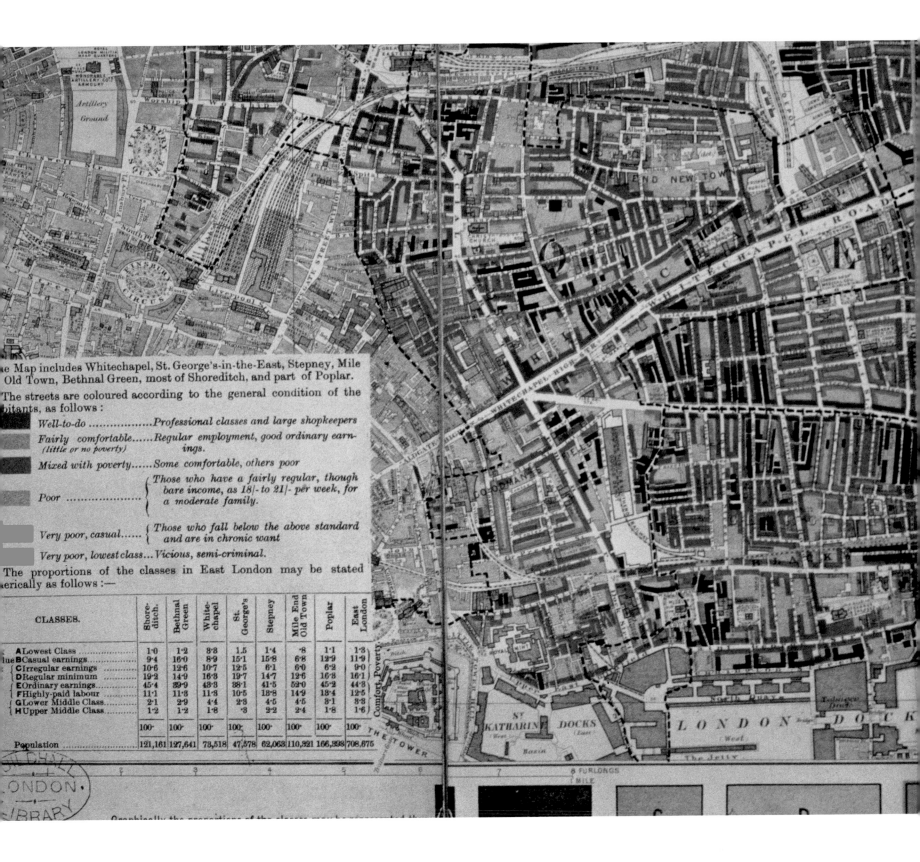

e Map includes Whitechapel, St. George's-in-the-East, Stepney, Mile Old Town, Bethnal Green, most of Shoreditch, and part of Poplar.

The streets are coloured according to the general condition of the bitants, as follows :

Well-to-do .... *Professional classes and large shopkeepers*

Fairly comfortable...... *Regular employment, good ordinary earn-*
(little or no poverty)   *ings.*

Mixed with poverty...... *Some comfortable, others poor*

Poor .... { *Those who have a fairly regular, though bare income, as 18/- to 21/- per week, for a moderate family.* }

Very poor, casual...... { *Those who fall below the above standard and are in chronic want* }

Very poor, lowest class... *Vicious, semi-criminal.*

The proportions of the classes in East London may be stated erically as follows :—

CLASSES.	Shore-ditch.	Bethnal Green	White-chapel	St. George's	Stepney	Mile End Old Town	Poplar	East London
A Lowest Class	1·0	1·2	3·3	1·5	1·4	·8	1·1	1·3
B Casual earnings.................	9·4	16·0	8·9	15·1	15·8	6·8	12·9	11·9
C Irregular earnings	10·6	12·6	10·7	12·5	6·1	6·0	6·2	9·0
D Regular minimum	19·2	14·9	16·3	19·7	14·7	12·6	16·3	16·1
E Ordinary earnings............	45·4	39·9	43·3	38·1	41·5	52·0	45·2	44·3
F Highly-paid labour	11·1	11·3	11·3	10·5	13·8	14·9	13·4	12·5
G Lower Middle Class..........	2·1	2·9	4·4	2·3	4·5	4·5	3·1	3·3
H Upper Middle Class..........	1·2	1·2	1·8	·3	2·2	2·4	1·8	1·6
	100·	100·	100·	100·	100·	100·	100·	100·
Population	121,161	127,641	73,518	47,578	62,063	110,321	166,393	708,675

Graphically the proportions of the classes may be represented th

Scenes from the London slums.

Top left dates from 1934-6; opposite left from 1956; the other photographs are from the nineteenth century. Poverty casts the same shadow.

Like any native population beggars had their particular beats or districts, and were identified by such. There were the 'Pye street beggars' and the 'St Giles beggars' while individuals did their own particular 'runs'. 'I always keep on this side of Tottenham Court Road,' a blind beggar confided to an investigator in the 1850s. 'I never go over the road; my dog knows that. I am going down there. That's Chenies-street. Oh, I know where I am; next turning to the right is Alfred-street, the next to the left is Francis-street, and when I get to the end of that the dog will stop.' So London can be mapped out through routes of supplication.

The beggars also learned the temperament of their fellow dwellers in the city. The rich and the middle class gave nothing at all, on the assumption that all beggars were impostors; this was of course the theme of official and quasi-official reports, which they willingly and gladly accepted. In a city beginning to be ruled by system, systematic prejudice also emerged. 'If the power of reasoning were universally allotted to mankind', wrote John Binny, the author of *Thieves and Swindlers*, 'there would be a poor chance for the professional beggar.' The more affluent sort of tradesmen were also immune to appeal. But beggars were successful 'amongst tradesmen of the middle class, and among the poor working people'. Their particular benefactors were the wives of working men, which corresponds to the testimony of others that the London poor were charitable to the poor whose need was greater than their own. It suggests also that, contrary to public opinion, not all beggars were impostors; there were some who summoned up fellow feeling.

Memoirs of the early twentieth century do not report bands or troupes of beggars, but specific individuals who customarily made a pretence of selling matches or lozenges as a cover for begging. They were required to own a 'hawker's licence', which cost five shillings a year, and then they selected their 'patch'. One, on the corner of the West End Lane and Finchley Road, used to wind up a gramophone; another used to wander along Corbyn Road with a single box of matches; there was an organ-grinder called 'Shorty' who used to 'work' Whitechapel and the Commercial Road. These are all stray cases, but they impart the flavour of London begging between the wars. The author of *London's Underworld*, Thomas Holmes, remarks: 'it is all so pitiful, it is too much for me, for sometimes I feel that I am living with them, tramping with them, sleeping with them, eating with them; I become as one of them.' It is the sensation of vertigo, of being drawn to the edge of the precipice in order to throw oneself down. How easy it must be to become one of them, and willingly to go under. This is the other possibility which the city affords. It offers freedom from ordinary cares, and all the evidence suggests that many beggars actually enjoyed their liberty to wander and to watch the world.

The sellers of bootlaces and matches have gone and in their place, in the twenty-first century, have come 'the homeless' who sleep in doorways; they carry their blankets with them as a token of their status. Some of them have all the characteristics of their predecessors; they are slow-witted, or drunken, or in some other way disabled from leading an 'ordinary' existence. Others are shrewd and quick-witted, and not unwilling to practise the old arts of shamming. But such cases, perhaps, form the minority. Others find that they are genuinely unable to cope with the demands of the city; they fear the world too much, or find it difficult to acquire friends and form relationships. What will the world of London seem to them then? It becomes a place which the dispossessed and homeless of all ages have experienced: a maze of suspicion, aggression and small insults.

This unseen world exists still in the early twenty-first century, although it has changed its outward form. The close-packed tenements of Stepney have gone, but the high-rise estates have taken their place. The 'hereditary casuals' have been replaced by those seeking 'benefit'. In Wellclose Square there was a mission designed to harbour 'the people nobody wants', the rejected and the discarded who would otherwise simply fade into the streets. They fade because nobody sees them. There are certain busy places of London, like the forecourt of Charing Cross Station, where lines of people queue for soup from a Salvation Army mobile canteen; but for the crowds hurrying past them, it is as if they were not there at all. A beggar can lie immobile among happy crowds of people drinking outside a pub, unacknowledged and unregarded. In turn these dispossessed people gradually lose all contact with the external world; and in London it is easier to go under than in any other part of the country. A recent survey of a night shelter in central London, reported in *No Way Home* by S. Randall, revealed that 'four fifths of young people . . . were from outside London and most were recent arrivals'; the city is, as ever, voracious. A quarter had been 'in care', half had already 'slept rough', and nearly three-quarters 'did not know where they were going next'. They were characteristically in ill health, with inadequate clothing and no money. This night shelter was at Centrepoint, beside the site of the old rookery of St Giles where previous migrants to London had lived in rags.

It has often been suggested that the East End is a creation of the nineteenth century; certainly the phrase itself was not invented until the 1880s. But in fact the East has always existed as a separate and distinct entity. The area of Tower Hamlets, Limehouse and Bow rests upon a separate strip of gravel, one of the Flood Plain gravels which were created at the time of the last glacial eruption some 15,000 years ago. Whether this longevity has played any part in creating the unique atmosphere of the East End is open to question, perhaps, but there is leisure to the West, and labour to the East. Yet in the early decades of the nineteenth century it was not singled out as being the most desperate source of poverty and violence. It was known principally as the centre of shipping, and of industry, and thus the home of the working poor. In fact the industry and the poverty steadily intensified; dye works and chemical works, manure factories and lamp-black factories, manufacturers of glue and of paraffin, producers of paint and bonemeal. In all this, of course, we see the condition of the sixteenth and seventeenth centuries being expanded and intensified; it is as if the process continued with a momentum of its own.

But then, at some point in the 1880s, it reached what might be called critical mass. It imploded. The East End became 'the abyss' or 'the nether world' of strange secrets and desires. It was the area of London into which more poor people were crammed than any other, and out of that congregation of poverty sprang reports of evil and immorality, of savagery and unnamed vice. In his essay 'On Murder, Considered as One of the Fine Arts', Thomas De Quincey apostrophised the area of the Ratcliffe Highway Murders of 1812 as one of the 'most chaotic' and 'a most dangerous quarter'. It is perhaps important that a writer should inscribe the East End in this manner, since its subsequent and lurid reputation was to a large extent established upon the work of journalists and novelists who felt almost obliged to conjure up visions of darkness and horror as a way of describing the shadow which London itself cast. And of course the defining sensation which for ever marked the 'East End', and created its public identity, was the series of murders ascribed to Jack the Ripper between the late summer and early autumn of 1888. The scale of the sudden and brutal killings effectively marked out the area as one of incomparable violence and depravity, but it was equally significant that the crimes should have been committed in the darkness of malodorous alleys. The fact that the killer was never captured seemed only to confirm the impression that the bloodshed was created by the foul streets themselves; that the East End was the true Ripper.

All the anxieties about the city in general then became attached to the East End in particular, as if in some peculiar sense it had become a microcosm of London's own dark life. There were books written, the titles of which represented their themes – *The Bitter Cry of Outcast London*, *The People of the Abyss*, *Ragged London*. In *Tales of Mean Streets* (1894) Arthur Morrison declared that 'There is no need to say in the East End of what. The East End is a vast city, as famous in its way as any the hand of man has made. But who knows the East End?'

The presence of 100,000 Jewish immigrants, in Whitechapel and in Spitalfields, only

poverty and overcrowding. The houses were small and narrow, while the streets themselves were often only fifteen feet wide. That sense of diminution, or of constriction, exists still. As the houses, so their inhabitants.

The industries of the eastern neighbourhood gradually became filthy, too. Much of its trade and commerce came from the river, but in the course of the seventeenth century the region became steadily industrialised. In the middle of the century Sir William Petty was lamenting 'the fumes, steams, and stinks of the whole Easterly Pyle', and indeed for hundreds of years after that the 'Easterly Pyle' became the home of what were known as 'the stink industries'; all forms of corruption and noisomeness were fashioned there. It represented the focus for London's fear of corruption and disease. Nor were these fears entirely ill-founded, either; demographic surveys revealed a remarkably high incidence of consumption and 'fever' in the eastern reaches of London.

So the flight westward continued. From the seventeenth century onward the laying out of streets and squares moved inexorably in that direction; the wealthy and the well-born and the fashionable insisted upon dwelling in what Nash called 'the respectable streets at the West end of the town'. The topographical divide, or rather the obsession with the West over the East, could be seen in minute particulars. When Jermyn Street was completed in the 1680s, the London Encyclopaedia observes that 'the west end of the street was more fashionable than the east.'

It has been observed that the West End has the money, and the East End has the dirt;

there is leisure to the West, and labour to the East. Yet in the early decades of the nineteenth century it was not singled out as being the most desperate source of poverty and violence. It was known principally as the centre of shipping, and of industry, and thus the home of the working poor. In fact the industry and the poverty steadily intensified; dye works and chemical works, manure factories and lamp-black factories, manufacturers of glue and of paraffin, producers of paint and bonemeal. In all this, of course, we see the condition of the sixteenth and seventeenth centuries being expanded and intensified; it is as if the process continued with a momentum of its own.

But then, at some point in the 1880s, it reached what might be called critical mass. It imploded. The East End became 'the abyss' or 'the nether world' of strange secrets and desires. It was the area of London into which more poor people were crammed than any other, and out of that congregation of poverty sprang reports of evil and immorality, of savagery and unnamed vice. In his essay 'On Murder, Considered as One of the Fine Arts', Thomas De Quincey apostrophised the area of the Ratcliffe Highway Murders of 1812 as one of the 'most chaotic' and 'a most dangerous quarter'. It is perhaps important that a writer should inscribe the East End in this manner, since its subsequent and lurid reputation was to a large extent established upon the work of journalists and novelists who felt almost obliged to conjure up visions of darkness and horror as a way of describing the shadow which London itself cast. And of course the defining sensation which for ever marked the 'East End', and created its public identity, was the series of murders ascribed to Jack the Ripper between the late summer and early autumn of 1888. The scale of the sudden and brutal killings effectively marked out the area as one of incomparable violence and depravity, but it was equally significant that the crimes should have been committed in the darkness of malodorous alleys. The fact that the killer was never captured seemed only to confirm the impression that the bloodshed was created by the foul streets themselves; that the East End was the true Ripper.

All the anxieties about the city in general then became attached to the East End in particular, as if in some peculiar sense it had become a microcosm of London's own dark life. There were books written, the titles of which represented their themes – *The Bitter Cry of Outcast London*, *The People of the Abyss*, *Ragged London*. In *Tales of Mean Streets* (1894) Arthur Morrison declared that 'There is no need to say in the East End of what. The East End is a vast city, as famous in its way as any the hand of man has made. But who knows the East End?'

The presence of 100,000 Jewish immigrants, in Whitechapel and in Spitalfields, only

The market of Petticoat Lane, in 1900. There has been a market in this area since the eighteenth century.

served to emphasise the apparently 'alien' quality of the neighbourhood. They served also to reinforce that other territorial myth which clung to the East End. Because it did indeed lie towards the east, it became associated with that larger 'east' which lay beyond Christendom and which threatened the borders of Europe. The name given to the dispossessed children of the streets, 'street-Arabs', offers some confirmation of this diagnosis. The East End was in that sense the ultimate threat and the ultimate mystery. It represented the heart of darkness.

    Yet there were some who came as missionaries into that darkness. As early as the 1860s men and women, impelled by religious or philanthropic motives, set up halls and chapels in the East End. Arnold Toynbee declared in one of his lectures to the inhabitants of Bethnal Green: 'You have to forgive us, for we have wronged you; we have sinned against you grievously'. The tone of supplication in Toynbee's remarks might also be construed as

one of anxiety that those, who had been so grievously treated, might react against the 'sinners' who betrayed them.

There was indeed much radical activity in the East End, with the members of the London Corresponding Society in the 1790s and the Chartists in the 1830s meeting in the mug houses and public houses of Whitechapel and elsewhere, in order to promote their revolutionary causes. A radically egalitarian and anti-authoritarian spirit has always been rising from the area, in terms of religious as well as political dissent (if in fact the two can be distinguished). In the eighteenth century the Ancient Deists of Hoxton espoused millennarian and generally levelling principles, and there is evidence of Ranters and Muggletonians, Quakers and Fifth Monarchy men, contributing to the general atmosphere of dissent. In the early decades of the twentieth century, the political ethic of the East End was dominated by 'municipal socialism'.

Yet the East End never 'rose up', as the civic authorities feared. It was always considered a potent ground for insurrection, as Oswald Mosley and his followers demonstrated in the 1930s, but like the rest of London it was too large and too dispersed to create any kind of galvanic shock. A more important revolutionary influence came, in fact, from the immigrant population. The communist and anarchist movements among the German and Russian populations have borne significant witness to the effect of the East End upon human consciousness. There was the celebrated Anarchists Club in Jubilee Street, among whose members were Kropotkin and Malatesta; opposite the London Hospital along Whitechapel High Street, a hall accommodated the fifth congress of the Russian Social Democratic Labour Party which ensured the pre-eminence of the Bolshevik Party. In a hostel in Fieldgate Street, Joseph Stalin was a welcome guest. Lenin visited Whitechapel on numerous occasions, and attended the Anarchists Club, while Trotsky and Litvinov were also frequent visitors to the area. The East End can in that sense be considered one of the primary sites of world communism.

Yet, despite all the drudgery and the poverty, the autobiographical reminiscences of East Enders themselves do not dwell upon monotony or hardship, but upon the sports and clubs and markets, the local shops and local 'characters', which comprised each neighbourhood. As one old resident of Poplar put it in a recent history of the area, *The East End Then and Now*, edited by W.G. Ramsey, 'It never occurred to me that my brothers and sisters and I were underprivileged, for what you never have you never miss.' This is the experience of the East End, and of all other impoverished parts of London, for those who live in them; the apparent deprivation and monotony are never realised, because they do not touch the inner

The staff of a Jewish tailor shop in the East End. Before them, there were Hugenot weavers in the old neighbourhoods; after them, the trade was taken over by people from Bangladesh.

Immigrants from the West Indies.
Above: Arriving at Victorian Station in the early 1950s. Right and middle: In Brixton and in the previously Jewish quarter around Petticoat Lane. Far right: Despite gloomy predictions, London has displayed remarkable powers to adopt and assimilate.

Southam Street, North Kensington, 1956. Today, the Notting Hill Carnival, of Trinidadian origin, takes place in mid-to late August, exactly as the old Bartholomew Fair at Smithfield did.

experience of those who are meant to be affected by them. Any emphasis upon the uniformity or tedium of the East End has in any case to be seriously modified by the constantly remarked 'merriment' or 'cheerfulness' of its inhabitants. There was 'a valiant cheeriness full of strength,' Blanchard Jerrold remarked after reciting a litany of sorrowful mysteries to be found upon the eastern streets, 'everywhere a readiness to laugh.' He also observed that 'The man who has a ready wit will employ his basket, while the dull vendor remains with his arms crossed.'

Thus emerged the figure of the Cockney, once the native of all London but in the late nineteenth and twentieth centuries identified more and more closely with the East End. This was the character heard by V.S. Pritchett with 'whining vowels and ruined consonants' and 'the hard-chinned look of indomitable character'. The creation of that chirpy and resourceful stereotype can in some measure be ascribed to another contrast with East End monotony, the music hall. The conditions of life in Whitechapel, Bethnal Green and elsewhere may have predisposed their inhabitants to violent delights; the penny gaffs and the brightly illuminated public houses are testimony to that, as well as the roughness and coarseness which were intimately associated with them. But it is also significant that the East End harboured more music halls than any other part of London – Gilbert's in Whitechapel, the Eastern and the Apollo in Bethnal Green, the Cambridge in Shoreditch, Wilton's in Wellclose Square, the Queen's in Poplar, the Eagle in the Mile End Road, and of course the Empire in Hackney, are just the most prominent among a large number which became as characteristic of the East End as the sweatshops or the church missions. By the mid-nineteenth century, the area roughly inclusive of the present borough of Tower Hamlets harboured some 150 music halls. In one sense the eastern region of the city was simply reaffirming its ancient identity. It has been mentioned before that two of the earliest London theatres, the Theatre and the Curtain, had been erected in the sixteenth century upon the open ground of Shoreditch; the whole region outside the walls became a haven for popular entertainment of every kind, from tea-gardens to wrestling matches and bear-baiting. So the music halls of the East End represent another continuity within the area, equivalent to its poor housing and to its 'stink industries'.

Yet in another sense the halls represented the extension and intensification of East End life in the nineteenth century. Many emerged and prospered in the 1850s – the Eagle Tea Gardens, the Effingham and Wilton's are of that period – by including burletta performances as well as variety acts and orchestral music. Among those who played here were the 'lions comiques', Alfred Vance and George Leybourne, who sang such Cockney songs as 'Slap Bang, Here We Are Again' and 'Champagne Charlie'. Vance in particular was known for his

London's East End became 'the abyss', and the murders ascribed to Jack the Ripper confirmed its dark and lurid reputation.

LONDON blacks: 207

'coster' songs written in a 'flash' or Cockney dialect, among them 'Costermonger Joe' and 'The Chickaleary Cove' where humour and bravado are easily mingled. Such songs as these became the folk songs of the East End, animated by all the pathos and diversity of each neighbourhood, charged with the circumstances and realities of the entire area. They remain powerful because they are filled with a real sense of place, as tangible as Artillery Lane or Rotherhithe Tunnel. In the halls the common elements of privation, and poverty, were lifted into another sphere where they became touched by universal comedy and pity; thus, for a moment at least, was misery transcended. It would not be too much to claim, in fact, that the halls provided a boisterous and necessary secular form of the Mass in which the audience were themselves identified and uplifted as members of a general community.

Left: Marie Lloyd, the music hall performer w̶ became the model of th̶ London Cockney.

Right: Queenie Lawrence, on stage at Gatti's Music Hall, painted by Walter Sickert.

London has always been a city of immigrants. It was once known as 'the city of nations', and in the mid-eighteenth century Addison remarked that 'when I consider this great city, in its several quarters, or divisions, I look upon it as an aggregate of various nations, distinguished from each other by their respective customs, manners, and interests.' The same observation could have been applied in any period over the last 250 years. It is remarked of eighteenth-century London in Peter Linebaugh's *The London Hanged* that 'here was a centre of worldwide experiences' with outcasts, refugees, travellers and merchants finding a 'place of refuge, of news and an arena for the struggle of life and death'. It was the city itself which seemed to summon them, as if only in the experience of the city could their lives have meaning. Its population has been likened to the eighteenth-century drink 'All Nations', made up of the remains at the bottoms of various bottles of spirit; but this is to do less than justice to the energy and enterprise of the various immigrant populations who arrived in the city. They were not dregs or leftovers; in fact the animation and enterprise of London often seemed to invade them and, with one or two exceptions, these various groups rose and prospered. It is the continuing and never-ending story. It has often been remarked that, in other cities, many years must pass before a foreigner is accepted; in London, it takes as many months. It is true, too, that you can only be happy in London if you begin to consider yourself as a Londoner. It is the secret of successful assimilation.

Fresh generations, with their songs and customs, arrived at least as early as the time of the Roman settlement, when London was opened up as a European marketplace. The

The music hall dancer, Sarah Brown. She was
charged with indecency, for wearing this
costume, and imprisoned for three months.

The audience seen from the stage. Music hall
was the most popular form of London
entertainment.

Thomas Brown noted of London in 1730 that 'to see the Number of Taverns, Alehouses etc. he would imagine Bacchus the only God that is worshipp'd there'. By 1870 there were some 20,000 public houses and beer shops in the metropolis, catering to half a million customers each day, reminiscent of 'dusty, miry, smoky, beery, brewery London'.

working inhabitants of the city might have come from Gaul, from Greece, from Germany, from Italy, from North Africa, a polyglot community all speaking a variety of rough or demotic Latin. By the seventh century, when London rose again as an important port and market, the native and immigrant populations were thoroughly intermingled. There was also a more general change. It was no longer possible to distinguish Britons from Saxons and, after the northern invasions of the ninth century, the Danes entered the city's racial mixture. By the tenth century the city was populated by Cymric Brythons and Belgae, by the remnants of the Gaulish legions, by East Saxons and Mercians, by Danes, Norwegians and Swedes, by Franks and Jutes and Angles, all mingled and mingling together to form a distinct tribe of 'Londoners'. A text known as IV Aethelred mentions that those who 'passed through' London, in the period before the Norman settlement, were 'men from Flanders, Pontheiu, Normandy and the Ile de France' as well as 'men of the emperor: Germans'.

In fact London has always been a hungry city; for many centuries it needed a permanent influx of foreign settlers in order to compensate for its high death-rate. They were also good for business, since immigration has characteristically been associated with the imperatives of London trade. Foreign merchants mingled here, and intermarried, because it was one of the principal markets of the world. On another level, immigrants came here to pursue their trades when denied commercial freedom in their native regions. And, again, other immigrants arrived in the city ready and able to take on any kind of employment and to perform those tasks which 'native Londoners' (given the relative nature of that phrase) were unwilling to perform. In all instances immigration corresponded to employment and profit; that is why it would be sentimental and sanctimonious to describe London as an 'open city' in some idealistic sense. It has acquiesced in waves of immigration because, essentially, they helped it to prosper.

There were, however, occasions of criticism. 'I do not at all like that city,' Richard of Devizes complained in 1185. 'All sorts of men crowd there from every country under the heavens. Each brings its own vices and its own customs to the city.' In 1255 the monkish chronicler Matthew Paris was bemoaning the fact that London was 'overflowing' with 'Poitevins, Provençals, Italians and Spaniards'. It is an anticipation of late twentieth-century complaints that London was being 'swamped' by people from Africa, the Caribbean, or Asia. In the case of the thirteenth-century chronicler there is an atavistic and incorrect notion of some original native race which is being displaced by others.

There was a period of sustained suspicion in the 1450s, when Italian merchants and bankers were condemned for usury. But the imbroglio passed, leaving only its rumours as

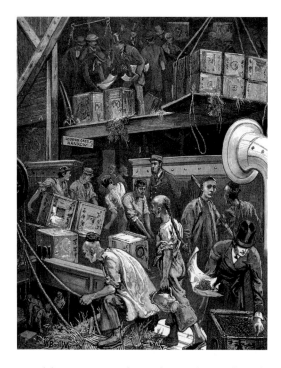

confirmation of the fact that Londoners were particularly sensitive to commercial double-dealing. The 'Evil May Day' riots of 1517, when the shops and houses of foreigners were attacked by a mob of apprentices, were dispelled with equal speed and without any permanent effect upon the alien population. This has been the custom of the city over many centuries; despite violent acts inspired by demagoguery and financial panic, the immigrant communities of the city have generally been permitted to settle down, engage with their neighbours in trade and parish work, adopt English as their native language, intermarry and bring up their children as Londoners.

Although the general number of European immigrants increased throughout the nineteenth century, the Jews and the Irish remained, as ever, the targets of public opprobrium. They were the object of derision and disgust because they lived in self-contained communities, popularly regarded as squalid; it was generally assumed, too, that they had somehow imported their disorderly and insanitary conditions with them. Philanthropic visitors to the Irish rookeries in Saint Giles in the fields discovered such scenes 'of filth and wretchedness as cannot be conceived'. Somehow these conditions were considered to be the fault of the immigrants themselves, who were accustomed to no better in their native lands. The actual and squalid nature of London itself, and the social exclusion imposed upon the Irish or the Jews, were not matters for debate. The question – where else are they to go? – was not put.

The popular prejudice against another Asian group is representative. By the late nineteenth century the Chinese, of Limehouse and its environs, were considered to be a particular threat to the native population. In the newspapers they were portrayed as both mysterious and menacing, while at a later date the dangerous fumes of opium rose in the pages of Sax Rohmer, Conan Doyle and Oscar Wilde. A cluster of associations was then reinforced. These particular immigrants were believed to 'contaminate' the surrounding urban population, as if the presence of aliens might be considered a token of disease. Throughout the history of London there has run an anxious fear of contagion, in the conditions of an overpopulated city, and that fear simply changed its form; the fear of pollution had become moral and social rather than physical or medical. In fact the Chinese were a small and

Left: On board a tea-ship.

Right: Workers on the London docks. The trade of the world flowed into London.

generally law-abiding community, certainly no more lawless than the residents by whom they were surrounded. The enclosed nature of the Chinese community in turn provoked a sense of mystery, and suspicions of evil; there was particular concern about the possibility of sexual licence in their 'dens of iniquity'. Once more these are characteristic of more general fears about immigration and resident aliens. They emanate in hostile attacks upon Russian Jews at the start of the twentieth century, against Germans during the world wars, against 'coloureds' in 1919. These anxieties were directed against Commonwealth immigrants in the 1950s and 1960s, and were in turn followed by hostility against Asian and African migrants in the 1980s and 1990s. The pattern changes its direction, but it does not change its form.

By the last decades of the nineteenth century London had become the city of empire; the public spaces, the railway termini, the hotels, the great docks, the new thoroughfares, the rebuilt markets, all were the visible expression of a city of unrivalled strength and immensity. It had become the centre of international finance and the engine of imperial power; it teemed with life and expectancy. Some of its gracefulness and variety had now gone; its Georgian compactness and familiarity had also disappeared, replaced by the larger scale of neo-classical or neo-Gothic architecture .

Late nineteenth-century London was established upon money. The City had acquired the historic destiny that it had been pursuing for almost two thousand years. It had become the progenitor of commerce, and the vehicle of credit, throughout the world; the City maintained England, just as the riches of the Empire rejuvenated the City. The sea trade of the earliest settlers had over the centuries borne unexpected fruit since by the turn of the century almost one half of the world's merchant shipping was controlled, directly or indirectly, by the institutions of the City.

The advent of electric light in the 1890s inevitably meant that natural light was no longer necessary to work indoors. So arrived those great waves of City workers who indeed might have been dwelling beneath the sea; they came to work in the darkness of a winter morning, and departed in the evening without once seeing the sun. So London helped to instigate one of the great disasters for the human spirit. In addition the use of new building technologies, particularly those of reinforced concrete and steel, and the introduction of passenger lifts, led inexorably to the erection of ever higher buildings. By that strange symbiotic process which has always marked the development of London, the expansion of the available space was matched only by the increase of the number of people ready to inhabit it. It has been estimated that the working population of the city numbered 200,000 in 1871, but 364,000 in 1911. Charles Pooter, of 'The Laurels', Brickfield Terrace, Holloway, is a fictional variant of one of the thousands of clerks who comprised what one guidebook terms 'a very city of clerks'. 'My boy, as a result of twenty-one years' industry and strict attention to the interests of my superiors in office, I have been rewarded with promotion and a rise in salary of £100.' The fact that the Grossmiths' comic creation has endured in public affection for more than a hundred years is testimony, perhaps, to the instinctive accuracy of their account; the ordinariness of Pooter's life was seen as emblematic of the new type of urban, or suburban man. In his loyalty, and in his naïveté, he was the kind of citizen whom London needed in order to sustain itself.

But it was not only a city of clerks. London had become the workplace of the new 'professions', as engineers and accountants and architects and lawyers moved ineluctably towards the city of empire. In turn these affluent 'consumers' created a market for new 'department stores' and new restaurants; there arose a revived and more salubrious 'West End' of theatres under such actor-managers as Irving and Beerbohm Tree. There were also more refined delights. The parks, the museums and the galleries of mid-Victorian London were discovered by a new and more mobile population of relatively affluent citizens. There were better libraries, and a plethora of distinguished or specialised exhibitions to satisfy a new urban taste for instruction compounded by enjoyment. It was also the city of Fabians, and of the 'new woman'; it was the home of the fin-de-siècle, most readily associated in the public mind with the spectacular London career of Oscar Wilde. But the old city never went away. In the 1880s approximately four hundred people of both sexes used to sleep in Trafalgar Square among the fountains and the pigeons.

In the Edwardian period London once more embodied a young and energetic spirit, with a curious acquisitive atmosphere which floods the pages of urban chroniclers such as H.G. Wells. The laborious and intricate city of the fin-de-siècle seems to have vanished, together with that heavy and lassitudinous atmosphere so peculiar to the memoirs of the period; it is as if the city had come alive with the new century. It was the first age of the mass cinema, too, with the advent of the Moving Picture Theatre and the Kinema. The Underground lines had abandoned their steam trains, and the whole network was electrified by 1902. Motor buses, tram-cars, lorries and tricycles added to the general momentum. London was, in a phrase of the period, 'going ahead'. One of the permanent, and most striking, characteristics of London lies in its capacity to rejuvenate itself. It might be compared to some organism which sloughs off its old skin, or texture, in order to live again. It is a city which has the ability to dance upon its own ashes. So, in the memoirs of Edwardian London,

Outside Mansion House looking down Cheapside. It remains one of the busiest junctions in the world.

Right: Ludgate Hill looking towards St Paul's. The route runs along the previous valley of the Fleet River which now flows underground beneath London's streets.

MAPPIN & W

CRITERION
CHARLES HAWTREY
TIME IS MONEY

PEARS

COLMANS
MUSTARD

London is always being re-built. Early photograph by Fox Talbot, dating from the 1840s.

there are accounts of *thés dansants*, tangos and waltzes and Blue Hungarian bands.

The Great War of 1914-18 cannot be said to have impeded the city's growth or its essential vitality. London has always been energetic and powerful enough to buttress itself against distress and disaster. London was accustomed to violence and to latent savagery, not least in the manifestations of the mob, and for many the vision of chaos and destruction acted as a restorative. The inhabitants of a large city are always the most sanguineous. It is true, also, that London expanded during the years of war. Just as in earlier centuries it had killed more than it cared for, so in the present conflict it seemed to thrive upon slaughter. The city's economy was fuelled by full employment, with so many of its young males detained else-where, and as a result the standard of living improved. Of course there were local hazards and difficulties. Building work was suspended, and at night the city was only partly illumi-nated by lamps which had been painted dark blue as a precaution against the raids of Zeppelin warships. But there were more foreign restaurants and pâtisseries than ever, as a result of the presence of émigrés, while the dance halls and music halls were full. There was a loss of life in the capital – it is still not unusual to find plaques upon the walls of long-since renovated buildings, commemorating a Zeppelin raid upon the site – with approximately seven hundred killed in the four years of war. In contrast it has been estimated that almost 125,000 Londoners died in battle. Yet London is prodigal of life.

The close of the war in November 1918 was greeted with scenes of revelry and enthu-siasm which have always punctuated the city's history. Stanley Weintraub has depicted the occasion in *A Stillness Heard Around the World: The End of the Great War*. 'The street was now a seething mass of humanity. Flags appeared as if by magic. Streams of men and women flowed from the Embankment . . . Almost before the last stroke of the clock had died away, the strict, war-straitened, regulated streets of London had become a triumphant pandemoni-um.' This is a description of the city stirring into life again, with the 'streams' of its citizens like the blood once more racing through its arteries. The celebrations there would continue for three days without ceasing. Paradoxically there was a certain amount of violence and riot to celebrate this peace, while one observer described it 'as a sort of wild orgy of pleasure: an almost brutal enjoyment. It was frightening. One felt that if there had been any Germans around, the women would have advanced upon them and torn them to pieces.' The same cru-elty had of course been visible in the crowd's delight at the beginning of the war. The frenzy spread in unexpected directions. There is the story of the famous parrot in the Cheshire Cheese Public House who with his beak 'drew a hundred corks without stopping amid the din of Armistice Night 1918 and then fell down in a faint'. It may seem perverse to pay more

these mingled landscapes. In the 1750s and 1760s, for example, villas emerged as standard suburban dwellings. They were soon visible in Islington and Muswell Hill, Ealing and Clapham, Walthamstow and South Kensington. It has been said that their example directly affected the appearance of a later and more extensive suburbia, with what John Summerson described as 'the flood of Victorian house-building, that torrent of "villadom"'. Yet the villas of the mid-eighteenth century anticipated the atmosphere and texture of later suburban life in more than an architectural sense. They embodied, for example, that privacy which was instinctive to the London character but which the city could no longer provide. One of the motives behind the movement towards the suburbs, both in its early and late forms, was to escape the sheer proximity of other people and other voices. The villas were originally designed as dwellings for one family, of course, surrounded and protected from the depredations of the city. The notion of one unit as one family is indeed central to the later

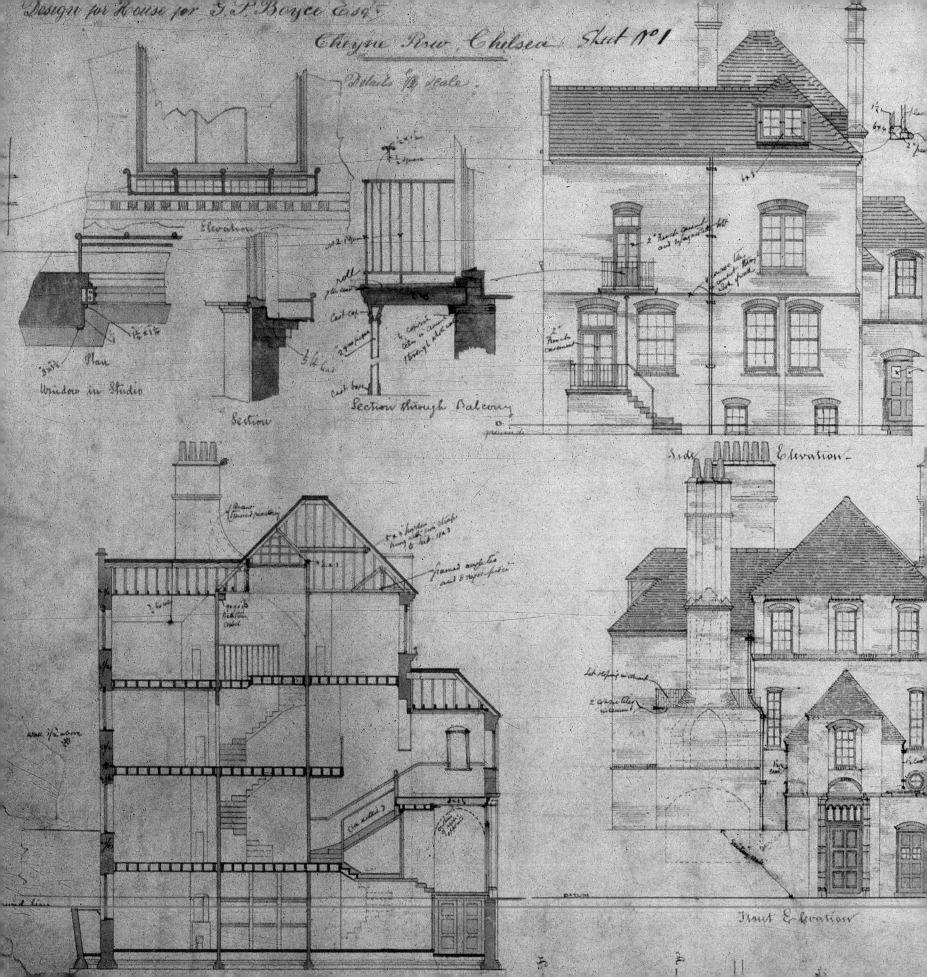

Design for House for G. P. Boyce Esq.

Cheyne Row, Chelsea — Sheet N° 1

Details ½ Scale

Elevation

Plan

Window in Studio

Section

Section through Balcony

Side Elevation

Front Elevation

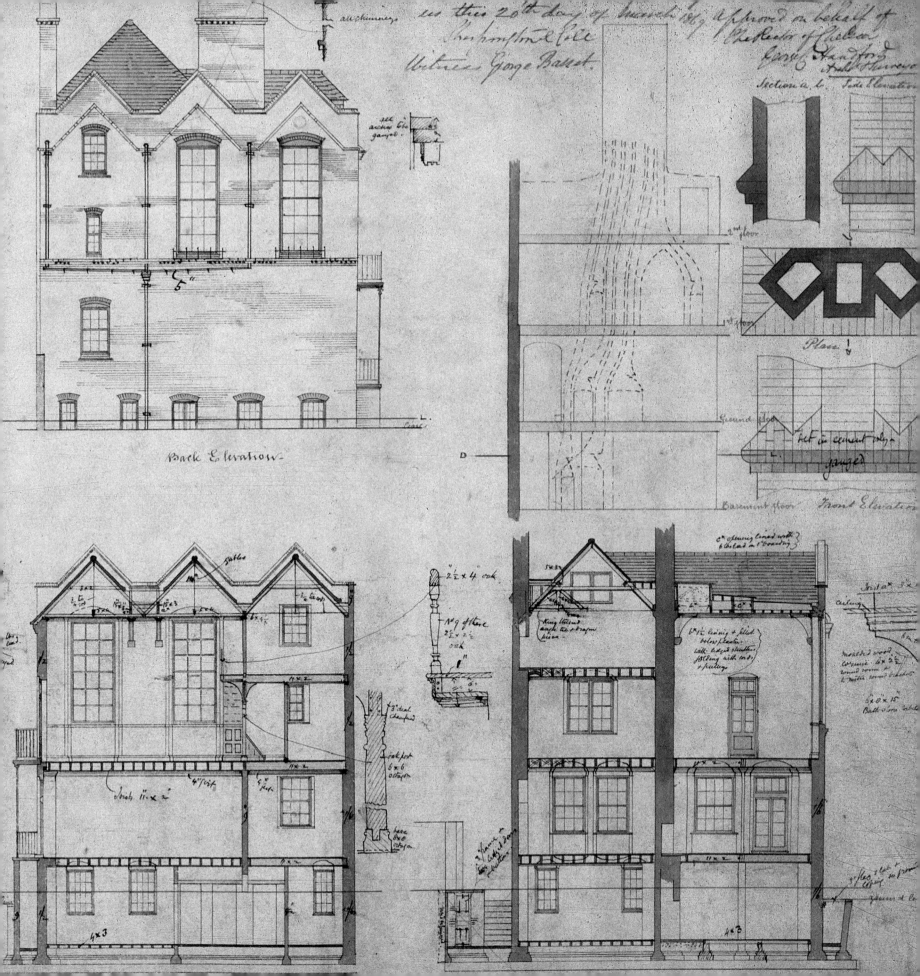

development of suburban life, where the yearning for safety and the relative anonymity of isolation have been equally powerful. The villas were 'detached'. Cheaper versions for the more populous areas were in turn established upon semi-detachment.

There are social, and aesthetic, consequences attendant upon what some might see as retreat or regression. The original villas were a highly visible token of respectability and this vision of respectability sustained the suburbs for the next two centuries. The phrase 'keeping up appearances' might have been coined for suburban living. But the original villas themselves introduced a form of artifice; they were not 'villas' in any classical sense, and the illusion of country living was sustained only with a great amount of determination and ingenuity. The nineteenth- and twentieth-century suburbs were also involved in an elaborate game of make-believe, with the implicit assumption that they were not part of the city at all. In reality they were as much an aspect of London as Newgate or the Tottenham Court Road, but their principal attraction was still based on the assumption that they were free of the city's noxious and contaminating influences.

This happy fiction could not be sustained for long, however, with the emergence of mass transport expediting the greatest exodus in London's history. Soon the pattern became clear, with the more prosperous citizens moving further out to more extensive grounds and

The expansion of London. Previous page: Designs by Philip Webb for Chelsea houses in Cheyne Row.

Above: A typical vista of surburban houses, neat and uniform.

Right: The development of a suburban estate at Ashburton in 1947.

eminences even as they were being displaced by new arrivals. The phenomenon is as old, and as new, as the city itself.

There was another characteristic urban process, too, with development along the lines of the main roads followed by a consolidation of the areas between the thoroughfares so that, as *The Builder* of 1885 put it, 'the growth of the solid nucleus, with but few interstices left open, has been nothing less than prodigious'. By the 1850s the city began to lose its population to areas such as Canonbury to the north, and Walworth to the south. The advent of cheap 'workmen's fares' meant that areas close to a railway station could be quickly inhabited; thus there emerged 'working-class' suburbs such as Tottenham and East Ham. The drift was gathering pace and by the 1860s the clerk and the shopkeeper desired nothing but a little villa 'out of town'.

In the mid-1930s it was estimated that, each day, two and a half million people were on the move in London. That is why there was a large increase in private, as well as public, suburbia. It was the age of 'Metroland', which began life with the Cedars Estate in Rickmansworth and spread outwards to include Wembley Park and Ruislip, Edgware and Finchley, Epsom and Purley. The importance of transport in effecting this mass dispersal is emphasised by the fact that the very notion of Metroland was created by the Metropolitan Railway Company, and heavily endorsed by the London Underground. Their booklets and advertisements emphasised the resolutely non-urban aspects of what were effectively great housing estates.

'Metroland beckoned us out to lanes in beechy Bucks', according to John Betjeman who had a tenacious if ambiguous affection for the suburban terrain – for 'gabled gothic' and 'new-planted pine', for the 'Pear and apple in Croydon gardens' and 'the light suburban evening' where a vast and welcoming security is so much to be hoped for. In a poem entitled 'Middlesex' Betjeman invoked another form of permanence – 'Keep alive our lost Elysium – rural Middlesex again' – and the advertisers of the Metropolitan Railway and the Underground exploited this ache, or longing, for continuity and predictability. According to the brochures – displaying, once more according to Betjeman, 'sepia views of leafy lanes in Pinner' – the new inhabitant of the suburbs will dwell beside 'brambly wildernesses where nightingales sing'. One advertisement prepared by the London Underground showed three rows of grey and mournful terraces, with the words 'Leave This and Move to Edgware'. A sylvan scene presents itself accompanied by a quotation from the seventeenth-century poet Abraham Cowley, who himself retired to Chertsey after the Restoration in 1660. In a single sentence he expresses the wish that 'I might be Master of a small House and a Large Garden, with moderate conveniences joined to them'. Once more the new suburban vision, in accordance with the implicit antiquarianism of London itself, took refuge in an appeal to an ill-defined and ill-explained past.

The same form of cultural nostalgia was evident in the architectural style of the new suburbs, the dominant model being 'mock Tudor' or what became known as 'Stockbroker Tudor' or 'Tudorbethan'. The desire was to combine the sense of continuity with the satisfaction of traditional workmanship and design. It was a way of conveying substantiality, and a measure of dignity, to these new Londoners who had exiled themselves from the central core of the city. The city can transform and regenerate itself in unanticipated ways. Thus the suburban Gardens, Drives, Parks, Ways and Rises are now as much a part of London as the old Rents and Lanes and Alleys.

London had created, and harboured, a new kind of life. Once more it happened unpredictably, with no concerted or centralised planning, and was directed by short-term commercial demands. So the suburbs became the home of shopping parades and imposing cinemas, of aesthetically pleasing Underground stations and ornate railway stations. It was the age of the Morris and the Ford. The factories which lined the new dual carriageways were now manufacturing the domestic items of this new civilisation – the washing machines and the refrigerators, the electric cookers and the wirelesses, the processed food and the vacuum

cleaners, the electric fires and the leatherette furniture, the 'reproduction' tables and the bathroom fittings. London is so ubiquitous that it can be located nowhere in particular. The extraordinary growth of its suburbs emphasised the fact that, since it has no defined or definite centre, its circumference is everywhere.

In *How Shall We Rebuild London?* C.B. Purdom, described the postwar city 'dulled by such extensive drabness, monotony, ignorance and wretchedness that one is overcome by distress'. That drabness or 'greyness', so characteristic in recollections of London in the 1950s, was a matter of privation; in the years immediately after the Second World War, most commodities were rationed. But in another sense it was the greyness of twilight. If one natural reaction after the war lay in the desire to create a 'new world', as the urban planners wished, then another was to reconstruct the old world as if nothing particular had happened. So when Roy Porter in *London: A Social History* invokes the 1950s in terms of a 'knees-up at the pub' and 'contented commuters', he is remarking upon the atavistic tendency of London to go on doing all the things which it had been doing before the unhappy interruption of hostilities. Yet it could not, and did not, succeed. The desire to impose a set of familiar conditions, in changed circumstances, led only to a vague atmosphere of oppression or constriction.

The two great set-pieces of London theatre were the Festival of Britain in 1951 and the Coronation of Elizabeth II in 1953. This sense of London as a successful and enthusiastic community, miraculously reassembled after the war, was subtly reinforced by the resurgence of orthodox values and conventional activities. Youth organisations, like the Scouts and the Cubs, flourished; it was a great period for Boys Clubs in east and south London. Attendance at football matches rose once again to prewar levels; the cinemas were also crowded, perhaps because, as one Londoner of the period recalled, 'there was practically nothing else to do'. This air of mild oppression, like a hangover after the excitement of war, was intensified by a concerted if unspoken desire to redefine sexual and social mores which had been considerably relaxed during the conflict. The relative sexual freedom of women, and the chummy egalitarianism of enforced contact between the classes, were phenomena strictly of the past. And that in turn led to further if ill-defined unease, especially among the younger population. The standards of the 1930s were being reintroduced within a quite different society. The imposition of two years of compulsory military service, known as 'National Service', only served to emphasise the atmosphere of general constriction. It was a less advantageous aspect of the newly formed 'welfare state'.

So London, then, was drab. Compared with other great cities, such as Rome and Paris

and New York, it was ugly and forlorn; for the first time in its history it had become something of an embarrassment. And yet there were already stirrings of change, arriving from unexpected quarters. The Teddy boys of Elephant and Castle, and other parts of south London, were joined by the bright young things of the Chelsea set and the beatniks of Soho, as objects of moral outrage. It is perhaps significant that these various groups were closely associated with certain areas of the city, as if local historical forces were also at work. Instead of those images of working-class youth in the late nineteenth and early twentieth centuries, shabbily dressed and with the uniform cloth cap perched upon their heads, there emerged a picture of boys in velvet jackets and drainpipe trousers. The recklessness and freedom, already evinced by the children of the Blitz, were still apparent. In the eighteenth and nine-teenth centuries clothes were 'handed down' from class to class in the spiral of trade, but on this occasion the disadvantaged actively promoted the transaction. It was another feature of native London egalitarianism accompanied by a self-possession and aggression which have been evident in London since the days of the medieval apprentices. In fact many Teddy boys were themselves apprentices.

London was becoming once more a young city. The rising birth rate and accelerating

Left: The Rolling Stones walking through Green Park, 1967. Licence was in the air.

Right: Crowds at a free 'pop concert' in Hyde Park, 1970.

Below: The crowds waiting to greet the Beatles, after they had received OBEs from the Queen in 1965.

prosperity of London in the 1950s helped to create a younger society which wished to divest itself of the limitations and restrictions of the postwar capital. There was no sudden transition, in other words, to the 'Swinging Sixties'. There were cafés and coffee bars and jazz-clubs in Soho; there were clothes-shops and small bistros in Chelsea some years before the efflorescence of boutiques and discothèques. London was slowly being rejuvenated, and by the mid-1960s it was suggested that 40 per cent of the general population were under twenty-five. This is approximately the condition of Roman London, when only 10 per cent of the population survived after forty-five, and we may infer a similar sexual energy. It also corresponds to the ratio of the city's population in the sixteenth century, where all the evidence suggests an earlier resurgence of the London appetite for fashion. If the conditions are approximately the same, then urban attitudes will be repeated.

In London, the 1960s were particularly charged with forgetfulness. The American weekly *Time* proclaimed on its front cover 'LONDON – THE SWINGING CITY'. Its affluence was visible enough; real earnings had risen by approximately 70 per cent in the twenty years since the war, and the high birth rate in the first years of peace certainly gave the impression of a city dominated by youth. The fact that National Service had been abolished in 1960 itself represented a literal and emblematic lifting of restrictions upon young males in

Estates in London – rising (above) and falling (right).

Battersea, 1969.

particular. So music, and fashion, returned on an unprecedented scale. One designer, Mary Quant, has suggested that she wished to create clothes that 'were much more for life – much more for real people, much more for being young and alive in'. So there was an efflorescence of boutiques in well-defined areas of London; Carnaby Street became the centre for young men who wore Mod fashions, with the familiar London emphasis upon what was 'new' or 'in the news', while the King's Road in Chelsea became the destination for young women who wished to be trendy. Music, too, emanated from London with groups such as the Who, the Kinks, the Small Faces and the Rolling Stones, many of their members having come from London art schools and colleges. Those groups from outside the city, like the Beatles, necessarily migrated to it. Designers had also caught the prevailing mood. Terence Conran recollected that 'I'd always believed that well-designed things should be available to the whole population, that it shouldn't be an elitist thing. And I think this coincided with a lot of people who'd had further education coming through who were discontented with the way things were.'

So broader access to higher education played its part in what Conran called 'the atmosphere of discontentment'. It was discontent, primarily, with the postwar world of hierarchy and repression but also with the perceived shabbiness and dreariness of London. It was a way of lightening the surroundings. The actual nature and identity of the city were no longer of any consequence. For a few years instead it became the 'style capital' where music and fashion attracted the ancillary industries of magazine publishing, photography, advertising, modelling, broadcasting and film-making to create a bright new city. But of course 'Swinging London' was not 'new' at all. The city's familiar instincts had never ceased their operation. The commercial imperative of the city's life, for example, had identified a 'market' among the newly resurgent youth which could be in turn exploited by intelligent entrepreneurs. The commercial infrastructure of the music business, for example, was already in place. In all areas of this teenage revolt, in fact, the youths themselves were exploited by a vast commercial project. It was a thoroughly London undertaking. The phenomenon of the 1960s was essentially theatrical and artificial in nature, too; like so many London displays, it glided over the fundamental underlying life in the capital. To see the decade clearly it is important to see it steadily, and as a whole, encompassing all of its realities.

It is significant, for example, that the age of the boutique and the discothèque was also the age of the tower block, of public vandalism, and of increased crime. They are not unconnected. Of the tower blocks of the 1960s, much has been written. They had become the resort of planners and architects motivated by aesthetic, as well as social, reasons. They seemed to offer the vision of a new kind of city; many Georgian and Victorian terraces were razed by the civic authorities to make way for an experiment in urban living in which a new kind of vertical community might be forged. The popularity of the tower blocks – some four hundred were erected in London during the late 1960s – was also animated by economic principles. They were standardised, and therefore could be quickly and cheaply assembled. There were so many people on housing lists, or living in parts of the 'inner city' which were deemed unfit for human habitation, that the 'high-rise estates' seemed at the time to be the only efficient and affordable means of translating citizens from relative squalor into relative comfort.

It was the age of the property developer when great fortunes could be made, trading off development land to the LCC for permission to build on sensitive sites. Their names were legion – Centrepoint, London Wall, Euston Centre, Elephant and Castle, all of London seemed to have been changed out of scale and out of recognition. It was a form of vandalism in which the government and civic authorities were happy to acquiesce. Vast swathes of London disappeared in the process – Printing House Square, Caledonian Market, St Luke's Hospital, parts of Piccadilly, stretches of the City, were all demolished in order to make way for what became known as 'comprehensive redevelopment'. What it represented was a deliberate act of erasure, an act of forgetting, not so dissimilar in spirit to the mood and ambience of the 'Swinging Sixties' elsewhere in London. It was as if time, and London's history, had for all practical purposes ceased to exist. In pursuit of profit, and instant gratification, the past had become a foreign country.

London has always been an ugly city. It is part of its identity. It has always been rebuilt, and demolished, and vandalised. That, too, is part of its history. The ancient creed – 'Cursed be he that removeth old landmarks' – has never been observed in the city. In fact one of the characteristics of London planners and builders, over the centuries, has been the recklessness with which they have destroyed the city's past. There were even songs on the subject from previous centuries:

> O! London won't be London long
> For 'twill all be pulled down
> And I shall sing a funeral song . . .

It might have been sung by Victoria Station, or Knightsbridge, or St Giles Circus, in the 1960s.

The haunts we revelled in today
We lose tomorrow morning,
As one by one are swept away
In turn without a warning . . .

In the 1260s all the old 'ruinated' work of past ages was swept away in the entire redevelopment of Bridge Ward. In the 1760s the medieval gates of the city walls were demolished on the grounds that they 'obstructed the free current of air'; in the same decade of 'improvement', houses were demolished to make way for new streets in no fewer than eleven wards. It was the greatest single change in London since the Great Fire a hundred years before. Then in 1860 the Union of Benefices Act expedited the destruction of fourteen city churches, some of them erected by Wren after that Fire. The 1860s were in fact the great period of destruction when, in the words of Gavin Stamp in *The Changing Metropolis*, 'half of London was being rebuilt . . . the city must have been a nightmare of dust, mud, scaffolding and confusion'. Queen Victoria Street and the Holborn Viaduct were being constructed, causing massive destruction to the oldest parts of London, while the various railway networks were defacing the cityscape with tracks and stations; the London Chatham & Dover Railway passed across Ludgate Hill, for example, and obscured the view of St Paul's Cathedral. This disfigurement of the cathedral was once more the charge levelled against property developers of the 1960s, so it would seem that there is no pause in the destruction of London. It can be no more than coincidence that these great waves of vandalism occurred in the 60s of each century, unless you were to believe that some theory of cyclical recurrence can be applied to the city's development. In that case we might expect the 2060s to mark the destruction of much twentieth-century building.

Other aspects of the 1960s seem, in retrospect, aligned to each other. There was an extraordinary and indeed unprecedented rise in crime, which tripled in the twelve years after 1955 and showed no signs of diminution in the late 1960s. The culture of instant

A Victorian tomb in a London cemetery. The angels have not quite disappeared.

'Punks' at a CND rally. London is a perennially youthful city.

The shining buildings of Docklands rise out of an erstwhile waste-land.

Olympia & York, was reduced to bankruptcy even as the tower was nearing completion. A third consortium took over the project, even though a surplus of office space in the rest of the capital mitigated against early success. And yet, somehow, it worked. Tenants were found, and the whole of Canary Wharf flourished.

Docklands itself experienced a similar fate. Wild fluctuations in the urban economy left it balancing between triumph and disaster on a number of occasions; its apartment blocks were fashionable one year, and unfashionable the next; there were complaints about rudimentary transport facilities as well as the absence of shops, but nevertheless there was continual development. Michael Hebbert, in London, has remarked that there were 'few preconceptions as to what should occur', and that this 'hands-off approach produced a curiously piecemeal environment'. Yet in that respect it followed the pattern of most London growth, which is no doubt the reason for its success.

The great tower of Canary Wharf, which dominates the London skyline, has won in Hebbert's words 'immediate acceptance and affection'. This great shaft, so in tune with the alignment of the city, now rivals the Monument and Big Ben as the symbol of London. It represents, too, the single most important shift in urban topography for many centuries; the commercial and social pressures had always edged westwards, but the development of Docklands has opened up what has been called London's 'eastward corridor' which in historical and structural terms offers passage and access to Europe at a time when London's economy is becoming more closely associated with the continent. There is a suspicion that the City of London – as well as the banks and brokers newly moved to Docklands – will come to dominate the financial markets of the European Community. Here, in this steady progress eastwards, we may be able to sense London's instinctive and almost primordial reaching towards money and trade.

It is appropriate to mention here the 'Big Bang' which transformed the City in the autumn of 1986; that explosion turned the Stock Exchange into the International Stock Exchange, enabled the merger of banking and brokerage houses, finished the system of fixed commissions and introduced 'electronic dealing'. It was not the beginning of the City's triumphalism; the phenomenon of young urban professionals named 'yuppies' had been first noticed in 1984: a group who, in the phrases of the period, wished to 'get rich quick' before 'burn-out'. But the events of 1986 heralded a sea-change in the position of the City of London. Its foreign exchange market is now the most advanced and elaborate in the world, handling approximately one-third of the world's dealings; with 600,000 employed in banking and allied services it has become the largest exchange in the world.

Yet the decade which saw the emergence of the 'yuppies', for example, also witnessed the revival of street-beggars and vagrants sleeping 'rough' upon the streets or within door-ways; Lincoln's Inn Fields was occupied once more by the homeless, after an interval of 150 years, while areas like Waterloo Bridge and the Embankment became the setting for what were known as 'cardboard cities'. The Strand, in particular, became a great thoroughfare of the dispossessed. Despite civic and government initiatives, they are still there. They are now part of the recognisable population; they are Londoners, joining the endless parade. Or perhaps, by sitting upon the sidelines, they remind everyone else that it is a parade.

And yet what is it, now, to be a Londoner? The map of the city has been redrawn to include 'Outer Metropolitan Areas' as well as 'Greater' and 'Inner' London; the entire south-east of England has – willingly or unwillingly – become its zone of influence. Is London, then, just a state of mind? The more nebulous its boundaries, and the more protean its identity, has it now become an attitude or set of predilections? On more than one occasion, in its history, it has been described as containing a world or worlds within itself. Now it has been classi-fied as a 'global city', and in Hebbert's words as 'a universe with its own rules, which has genuinely burst out of national boundaries'. So it does truly contain a 'universe', like some dense and darkly revolving cloud at its centre. But this is why so many millions of people describe themselves as 'Londoners', even if they are many miles from the inner city. They call themselves Londoners because they are pervaded by a sense of belonging. London has been continuously inhabited for over two thousand years; that is its strength, and its attraction. It affords the sensation of permanence, of solid ground. That is why the vagrant and the dis-possessed lie in its streets; that is why the inhabitants of Harrow, or Croydon, call themselves 'Londoners'.

It is in the nature of the city to encompass everything. So when it is asked how London can be a triumphant city when it has so many poor, and so many homeless, it can only be suggested that they, too, have always been a part of its history. Perhaps they are a part of its triumph. If this is a hard saying, then it is only as hard as London itself. London goes beyond any boundary or convention. It contains every wish or word ever spoken, every action or gesture ever made, every harsh or noble statement ever expressed. It is illimitable. It is Infinite London.